Counselling and Psychotherapy in Private Practice

PROFESSIONAL SKILLS FOR COUNSELLORS

The *Professional Skills for Counsellors* series, edited by Colin Feltham, covers the practical, technical and professional skills and knowledge which trainee and practising counsellors need to improve their competence in key areas of therapeutic practice.

Titles in the series include:

Medical and Psychiatric Issues for Counsellors
Brian Daines, Linda Gask and Tim Usherwood

Personal and Professional Development for Counsellors
Paul Wilkins

Counselling by Telephone
Maxine Rosenfield

Time-Limited Counselling
Colin Feltham

Long-Term Counselling
Geraldine Shipton and Eileen Smith

Client Assessment
Stephen Palmer and Gladeana McMahon (eds)

Counselling, Psychotherapy and the Law
Peter Jenkins

Contracts in Counselling
Charlotte Sills (ed.)

Counselling Difficult Clients
Kingsley Norton and Gill McGauley

Learning and Writing in Counselling
Mhairi MacMillan and Dot Clark

Referral and Termination Issues for Counsellors
Anne Leigh

Counselling and Psychotherapy in Private Practice

Roger Thistle

SAGE Publications
London • Thousand Oaks • New Delhi

First published 1998

SAGE Publications Ltd
6 Bonhill Street
London EC2A 4PU

SAGE Publications Inc.
2455 Teller Road
Thousand Oaks, California 91320

SAGE Publications India Pvt Ltd
32, M-Block Market
Greater Kailash—I
New Delhi 110 048

British Library Cataloguing in Publication data

A catalogue record for this book is
available from the British Library

ISBN 0 7619 5104 0
ISBN 0 7619 5105 9 (pbk)

Contents

Acknowledgements

I would like to express my thanks to those who have assisted me in writing this book. Friends, colleagues, practitioners and other people's clients have responded generously with their time, completing questionnaires and freely sharing their ideas and experiences. It was particularly useful to speak to those who had been in the role of practitioner and client simultaneously. My own clients and supervisees obviously cannot be named for reasons of confidentiality, however, I need to point out that this book could not have been written without them. I hope I have been of some help to most of the people I have seen over the past eleven years but whether this is true or not they have provided me with a rich experience of the clinical and practical issues pertaining to private practice. My supervisor David Richardson while keeping my work on the straight and narrow has also helped to mould my ideas about private practice. Ben Scott FCA has helped me review the chapters covering the financial aspects of self employment. Colin Feltham, my editor, has been infinitely patient and encouraging as has Susan Worsey at Sage and I am also grateful to the British Association for Counselling for their permission to re-print their Code of Ethics and Practice.

Lastly, I would like to thank my wife Marie and my children for their patience when I was spending more time with my word processor than with them!

Introduction

For some, starting up in private practice as a counsellor or psychotherapist will be a step towards a successful career, for others it will be a financial mistake. Some practitioners will jog along, receiving a reasonable financial return for their efforts, while others will be highly successful, both financially and in the professional reputation that they develop. If you have undergone a substantial training in counselling or psychotherapy, and are committed to professional development while seeking a fresh challenge, then you may be considering starting up your own private practice. Or perhaps you are already seeing clients privately but are wondering how to expand or become more successful. Be assured that this book was written by someone who has had to face many of these challenges in the course of his practice. Whether you earn, or you are planning to earn an income from working privately as a counsellor, counselling psychologist, clinical psychologist, psychotherapist or psychoanalyst, this book will be relevant to your circumstances.

I came to write this book because my working life to date has had two major strands, namely finance and counselling. I grew up in a family where my father was a tax consultant and my mother, aunt and uncle were all bankers. I too spent ten years in banking, credit approval and financial marketing. These experiences provided the financial background I needed when, twelve years ago, I changed career, retrained as a counsellor and developed a private counselling practice and related consultancies.

There is of course a lengthy debate that could be had about the differences and the similarities between counselling, counselling psychology, psychotherapy and psychoanalysis. Offering long-term therapy rather than short-term counselling may well provide a more steady income for the practitioner, but this is not necessarily the case. Most psychotherapists would probably admit to having some clients who leave after one or two sessions and many counsellors continue seeing clients for several years. Differences between these professions are largely not relevant to the success of a private practice and so are not explored further in this book. Of course this does not mean you should deliberately blur the differences. It is important that you are clear about the training which you have undertaken and that you only work within your capabilities for it would be unethical to do otherwise.

There has been a relatively slow growth in articles (Blower and Rink, 1987) and books on private practice in counselling and psychotherapy in the UK (Coltart, 1993; Syme, 1994; McMahon, 1994). My purpose in writing this book is to pass on some practical experiences, explaining how it is possible to integrate an ethical and caring approach to clients with a businesslike attitude to work. Potentially there are many pitfalls for people working outside institutional settings, but it is perfectly possible to develop a professional practice that delivers income, variety of work and most importantly satisfied clients. The issues of appropriate training, supervision, qualification, accreditation or registration and personal therapy are essential considerations for any counselling or psychotherapy practitioner.

Other matters that I have covered include planning and research, marketing, accounting, tax matters, premises, legal issues, in fact everything that helps build a successful business. This book should be of interest to those who are already in training or wondering about beginning; those who want to plan their career; those who wish to weigh up their prospects of establishing a private practice and those wanting to improve an existing one.

1

You and Private Practice

What is private practice?

What exactly is meant by the term 'private practice' as it relates to counselling and psychotherapy? In this book I refer to 'practitioners', by this term I mean mainly counsellors and psychotherapists, who earn all or part of their income directly from their clients, working professionally in the context of a therapeutic relationship.

Such practice is private in the sense that it is not publicly funded (such as the NHS and social services). Consequently services are not generally free to clients. Practitioners are self-employed people, responsible for generating their own income and managing their own businesses although they may co-operate with others, establish formal partnerships with individuals or organisations or have other sources of income including part-time employment.

Such a working arrangement means that there is a direct and confidential business relationship between each practitioner and their clients, usually based on a contract which is either formal or a verbal agreement between them (Sills, 1997). People working for themselves are not employed as such, neither are they managed (by an individual or an organisation). This means they are responsible primarily to their clients although they may well belong to professional bodies which expect certain standards from them. This independence allows for freedom of operation and methods. However, with freedom comes responsibility and there is always a risk that anyone working in isolation might overcharge, offer a poor service or abuse their clients in any other way.

Science and ethics

While such treatment seems to be of benefit to many, opponents point out that there is no scientific proof of effective treatment (Eysenck, 1992). This contrasts with the medical world, where for example, there is clear evidence of patient recovery following drug treatment. Counselling and psychotherapy rely on general theories and practices established over time and an impression that most clients feel better following treatment. Some researchers, however, are now confident that the case for the effectiveness of counselling and psychotherapy has been firmly made (Smith et al., 1980).

Without scientific proof these professions remain vulnerable to criticism. For example, in general medicine, doctors and their patients are protected by the British Medical Association which lays down clear ethical standards for treatment, whereas counsellors and psychotherapists may choose to belong to one of a wide range of training or professional bodies or to none at all.

This split between medical and psychological treatment can be traced back to differences of approach among the founders of the professions. There has always been controversy over whether psychoanalysis was a profession which should only be staffed by qualified medical practitioners or whether it was possible for non-medically trained people to become equally proficient.

In the late nineteenth century, Sigmund Freud found himself at the centre of this challenge from the medical profession. In more recent times there has been some serious thinking about the ethical basis for people advertising themselves and working in private practice as counsellors or psychotherapists. Today there is a recognition that poor quality practitioners cast a shadow on the profession as a whole and this has led to the formation of professional bodies with defined codes of ethics and practice for their members, including the power to investigate complaints from clients.

This type of work requires life experience, so it is not suited to school or college leavers or those with little experience of adult life and human relationships. Some practitioners do come from a background of health care but there are many other routes which lead into this kind of work, including teaching, education, personnel management, social work and the churches. Some choose counselling or psychotherapy as a completely new career in mid-life, perhaps after a positive experience of undergoing personal therapy for themselves. While lack of life experience means that it is not a suitable career for the very young, it has been known for people who have retired to train and set up in private practice.

Despite attempts to introduce legislation and professional registers, currently anyone may operate as a counsellor or psycho-therapist in the UK with no training, no qualifications, and without registering with any organisation. The respected professional bodies would regard this as an unethical thing to do, but it is not illegal. This is because it involves the acts of talking and listening and it is really quite difficult to design legislation which accurately defines the differences between analysis, psycho-therapy, counselling, listening and befriending. (For a detailed discussion of the arguments see Jenkins, 1997.) For several years the bodies that have attempted to regulate these professions have wrestled with their differences and been unable to arrive at a common definition of acceptable practice. This is hardly surprising when counselling and psychotherapy appear to do very similar things and yet are regarded by many of their own practitioners as different professions (James and Palmer, 1996). However, there are now real attempts to co-ordinate registration of counsellors and psychotherapists through the United Kingdom Council of Psychotherapy Register and the United Kingdom Register of Counsellors. At the same time, there is a backlash by those unhappy with over-professionalisation (Mowbray, 1995).

There is a wide spectrum of training courses available within the fields of counselling, psychotherapy and psychoanalysis. This ranges from evening classes in basic counselling skills to courses over several years for those training as psychoanalysts. While some practitioners will work without charge in voluntary settings others will charge Harley Street type fees comparable with any private medical practitioner. Practitioners cover a wide range of therapies including marriage and couple work, family, group, art, and drama therapy, behavioural and cognitive therapists, bereavement and trauma counsellors and so on.

Despite strenuous attempts to lay ground rules it is clear that no one body of professionals can as yet lay claim to a single definition of the 'talking cure' which embraces all aspects of counselling and psychotherapy practice. It is difficult, if not impossible, to arrive at a clear definition for elements of counselling and psychotherapy are practised in a whole range of other jobs as well, such as social work, teaching, psychology, psychiatry and religious ministry. Many people simply use counselling skills within their work. Others who are simply good listeners use this in everyday life and relationships and do not regard it as anything professional at all. For a full discussion of these issues see Feltham (1995a).

By definition therefore, there must be as many types of private practice as there are private practitioners. Because private practice is a confidential arrangement between two people and (at least in one-to-one work) there is no third party involved, it has to be based upon trust and so inevitably carries some risk that one person may abuse the other. Clients may be less likely to ask about qualifications than a potential employer, so working privately may be used unethically by some practitioners as a means of disguising a lack of qualifications. Certain political objections to private practice have also been advanced by Pilgrim (1993; 1997).

Having said that, there are many people who derive great satisfaction from providing a well run, ethical and successful private practice and many clients who appreciate the private, anonymous or confidential setting (Feltham, 1995b).

Would private practice suit me?

All potential practitioners need the ability to listen to their own needs and this is a particularly important exercise to undertake before entering the world of private practice. It can be difficult to do this alone, and even if you are undergoing personal therapy yourself you may feel it is difficult to raise such topics within the course of the therapy. Consider discussing your ideas with a trusted friend, a colleague or another practitioner but for a truly objective view don't choose somebody nearby that you may eventually be competing with for clients! Probably you have already asked yourself why you want to do this kind of work, but why specifically do you want to work privately?

Look at the questions below as a starting point. Try to have a really honest dialogue with someone whose judgement you trust:

- Will it suit me to be alone with my clients for much of my week, or would I be happier in a partnership or a centre working with colleagues?
- Will I be aiming to work full-time or part-time?
- Do I need variety in my week, such as lecturing, supervising or other kinds of work that are unconnected with therapy?
- Can I afford to risk being entirely reliant upon my clients for my income?
- Do I have other interests outside the world of therapy that enrich the quality of my life?
- Does my training equip me to work in private practice?
- Is there likely to be a demand for services in the area where I plan to work?
- Am I prepared to promote myself and my practice in order to find sufficient clients?
- Will private practice fit in with my family or other relationships?
- How do I feel about the politics of private practice, especially charging people money for my time?
- How would my needs for supervision change if I were to work in this way?
- Do I have the use of suitable premises?

Be as objective as you can in answering these questions, and think these things through carefully because not everyone has a personality suited to private practice. It is better to be clear in advance whether it is right for you. If you are the sort of person who likes plenty of company, good job security, regular working hours, and prefers to keep work and home life completely separate, then you may want to think again. A private practice can be lonely and isolated unless you put in place regular breaks, a variety of work, quality supervision, and a good support network which offers the opportunity to meet regularly with other practitioners.

Getting these ideas clear from the start can save a lot of problems later. Are you planning to make as much money as you can from your practice or are you offering counselling as a service to the community? Or, like many practitioners, do you accept that some clients will be able to pay 'in full' while others will never be able to do so? Is your aim to bring in a little extra income on top of another job, or will this be your only source of income to support a family and see you through to retirement?

For many people starting up in private practice it makes sense to see some private clients, but work part-time somewhere else such as a counselling centre, GP practice, helpline or employee assistance programme. Having other regular work reduces reliance on private clients for income. This may be particularly important in the early stages as a practice becomes established. It also creates the opportunity to meet regularly with a group of colleagues. Talking to others as I wrote this, I was struck by the number of occasions on which professional isolation was mentioned as a problem for private practitioners. In addition to formal supervision arrangements, peer groups can offer mutual support and (provided confidentiality is respected) somewhere to unburden yourself informally after a difficult client session. Having such a place to share professional concerns can be a positive benefit to the practitioner who at other times works alone.

Working for yourself

Have you ever worked for yourself before? If you have, you will know how important it is to be self disciplined about your day. You will only make a living if you are prepared to be single-minded about your business. Whether you see a couple of clients each week or you have a busy full-time practice, you will want to provide an ethical, caring service for your clients, but you will also need to ensure that your costs do not exceed your income, that you are efficient when it comes to chasing up unpaid bills and that you maintain a regular flow of cash.

When I decided to train full time as a counsellor, I was not entitled to a grant so I had to support myself and my family throughout my training. A nine-to-five job was out of the question because it would clash with the times of my seminars and yet I would also need to be available to see clients in the evenings. I needed a part-time job with flexible hours that would provide a regular income for up to three years, so I ran a small gardening business, offering turfing, weeding and general tidying. I placed a simple small ad in the local free paper and soon I was inundated with customers.

I had never intended that this work would be permanent, but it not only provided a modest income while I studied, but also proved to be a good balance to the intellectual and emotional stimulation of a psychodynamic counselling diploma training programme. It also gave me first-hand experience of business planning and budgeting. Some of the older and more lonely customers would use my coffee breaks to talk about their problems, which helped confirm that counselling was the career I wished to follow. Fellow students came from a range of backgrounds. Some already qualified in mental health nursing were able to cover night duties at a local psychiatric hospital while studying. A GP's receptionist was already providing informal counselling to patients when she decided to train. Consider therefore whether you have existing skills which could support you financially through training and the early years of a developing practice.

Some people are attracted to self-employment because they want to be their own boss, imagining that it would be a great relief to have no-one telling them what to do every day. This is not a good enough reason in itself however.

Annie was a social worker who felt unsupported at work. She frequently felt that she could do a better job offering counselling on her own. She was a caring and sympathetic person by nature, but found self-assertion difficult, in particular when it came to handling money. She advertised for clients and was quite successful in getting them but when it came to charging them she set her fees at a very low level and found it difficult to collect unpaid bills. She gave up after a year because she couldn't make ends meet and is now back in social work where she gets a regular salary and leaves her union to do the negotiating.

Rather than escape from the control of one boss, like Annie you may well find you end up with many bosses, for it is your clients who will be paying you and effectively hiring or firing you.

To be self-employed you also need to be a self-starter, someone who is well motivated, able to start work on time and motivated to provide an excellent service. If you don't believe in what you are doing and are not able to provide a high quality of service, your professional reputation will soon vanish along with your clients. If you don't believe that you are worth the fees that you are charging, you will have difficulty in invoicing your clients at a rate that will sustain your business.

Personal therapy

Do you need to be in regular personal therapy if you are to offer therapy to others? You should consider this question from two perspectives, both during training and then afterwards. Many counselling courses require their students to be receiving therapy for themselves at least once a week during their training. It is not normally regarded as a condition for future practice of cognitive or behavioural therapy, but psychotherapy or analytic training usually requires the experience of twice a week or more frequent personal therapy. This may well be a requirement from well before the start of the actual training programme.

While it is perfectly possible to use a trusted and more experienced colleague who has experienced a similar training, a much richer experience is likely where trainees and their therapists have different experiences of training, but who are at the same time respectful of each other's background. One training institute wrestled for years with the problem of finding external therapists who understood their way of working. This became a real problem as the institute matured. If they recommended internally trained people as training analysts, they could be open to criticism that they were a narrow and incestuous organisation, insufficiently open to outside influence. If however they recommended external ones to their trainees, what did this say about the quality of their own graduates? For some time they got around the problem by holding a list of approved therapists taken from a list of other reputable training organisations. All was well until their own graduates started to ask why they were not being considered for the list! A compromise was reached by establishing criteria for qualifying their own mature graduates as training therapists.

Some practitioners such as cognitive or behavioural therapists may not regard personal therapy as necessary at all. To psychodynamic counsellors and psychotherapists who ask whether they can end their personal therapy once they have finished their training, the answer is that if they need to ask they doubtless need to continue! There may be times in life when you can practise perfectly adequately without personal therapy provided that you are receiving regular supervision of your casework. But it is important to listen to what your supervisor has to say on this. If your supervisor recommends that you examine a particular aspect of your work in therapy this does not necessarily mean several more years of therapy. It may be possible to undertake a piece of focused work on a single issue.

Others choose to remain in a permanent therapeutic relationship as well as supervision. Issues presented in personal therapy and supervision do of course overlap at times, but having access to both provides two distinct places in which to reflect. Supervision offers a protection for clients and focuses on the interaction with the practitioner, while personal therapy or analysis provides wider opportunities for personal growth and self-awareness which inevitably impacts upon work with clients.

Remember as a self-employed person you will not be subject to the same disciplinary and management structures as an employee. Consequently, it is all the more important to give serious consideration to your own need for personal therapy as well as other means of continuing personal and professional development (Wilkins, 1997).

The need for supervision

Supervision should not be simply an option from time to time. Because psychotherapy training takes place over a lengthy period and on some courses requires intensive personal analysis several times a week, students may feel or even be told at the end of their course that supervision is for students only and no longer necessary once the training is complete. This is a rather dangerous assumption, for no-one can predict with accuracy the future state of mind of another person. The British Association for Counselling (BAC) for example stipulates that for its members, career-long supervision is mandatory not optional. Bereavement, relationship difficulties and other emotional problems can of course befall practitioners just as much as the rest of the population. Indeed, it might be argued with some justification that because many practitioners enter counselling or psychotherapy practice out of painful personal experiences they are even more likely than the average person to need help themselves in the future. It is of course the positive aspect of this that we draw upon in order to enhance empathic responses to our clients, but there is no doubt that without good quality and regular supervision we may never hope to separate our own feelings and responses from the objective needs of our clients.

Supervision protects clients. It is all too easy to allow prejudices and projections to affect quality of work unless we are open to the impartial examination and reflection which supervision provides. Practitioners for their own benefit also find it important to have someone to talk to about their work. People working in private practice are vulnerable to loneliness and isolation; rather more so than those who work for agencies where there is plenty of opportunity to discuss casework with colleagues.

Who to use for supervision?
Finding the right supervisor is an extremely important step, for a good one will help you and your practice to grow and mature while an inadequate supervisor may have the opposite effect. Poor quality supervision, especially in the early years of practice can be demoralising or even destructive. Some students moving into private practice, with little income and few clients have been tempted to use their personal therapist for supervision. Although this may work well on occasions, it fails to provide an objective view of the client's needs which is crucial to supervision. Others have chosen a supervisor already familiar with their work as a student; perhaps a lecturer from college. This too has its drawbacks. Such a relationship may keep the practitioner a perpetual student, preventing growth or confident exploration of new ideas, theories and practice. Although not ideal, as a starting point it at least provides a familiar environment and there may be compensating benefits in having trust in one another's professional background.

However, a supervisor should provide added value to your work with clients, stretching and at times challenging your established practice. For example, if you are trained only in seeing clients individually, but consult a supervisor who has training and experience in couples work, this may provide an added dimension to your work. This does not of course mean that you should promote yourself as capable of client work for which you are unqualified, but it can widen your thinking about your clients and provide a better understanding of other styles of work. In turn this will broaden your experience and clarify those areas where you could seek further training.

A supervisor's background should not be so different from yours that they lack any understanding of, or respect for, your methods. A supervisor with a cognitive approach to problem solving may not be the best person with whom to discuss transference issues. But then neither might it be helpful, when faced with a client who had experienced a terrorist incident, to be told to interpret the client's past life experiences when they simply needed to make supported visits to the place where the incident occurred.

Some matters such as appropriate boundary setting are common to private practice whatever your specific training. Probably your supervisor should be someone who has had experience of private practice. However, private practitioners often move on to become supervisors as they gain experience, so you should not necessarily expect their experience of private clients to be current. When considering in depth how to approach a new supervisor, consult Carroll (1996) and Shipton (1997).

Psychiatric consultancy

In private practice there is always the chance that a client with serious mental health problems will find their way to your practice. So, in a addition to a supervisor it is good practice also to have access to a qualified psychiatrist who can provide both advice to you and when necessary a mental health assessment for your client. Ideally, such a consultant psychiatrist should be in a position to obtain prompt access to psychiatric hospital beds and be able to prescribe medication. Having a pre-arranged professional consultancy like this makes it easier to deal promptly with a client who is giving you cause for concern, whether you are meeting for the first or for subsequent sessions.

On occasions you may wish to make it a condition that a client undergoes a psychiatric assessment, especially if you consider that their mental health will prevent them from benefiting from the level of service you can offer. Sadly, people who are not properly qualified sometimes continue to see clients under such circumstances, even when their state of mental health makes them unlikely to benefit. In such cases it is more ethical to make a referral to a psychiatrist and even if the client refuses to go you may need to consider (in discussion with your supervisor) how you sensitively withdraw from the work. A seriously disturbed individual is unlikely to benefit from therapy at least until they have acknowledged the limitations of their illness and sought appropriate treatment. On some occasions it will be sufficient to refer a disturbed client to their own GP with the recommendation that they should be passed on to local psychiatric services. Some therapists may have special training and aptitude for working with such clients. One of the best ways of gaining experience in this area of work is by attending ward rounds and case discussions within a local psychiatric hospital. There may be opportunities to do this independently or as a work placement during a recognised training course. Serious applicants are often welcomed as honorary counsellors or psychotherapists within an NHS psychiatric team as their input can enable more patients to be seen.

Practitioners report occasions when clients are too ill to make contact with a doctor or psychiatrist and need to be personally escorted to hospital, to a psychiatric social worker or even in extreme cases, to the police. It is important to be prepared for such eventualities for although rare they can be distressing and very time consuming. (See the section in Chapter 6, Safety, Boundaries, Insurance and Private Practice.)

Resource index

Before you take your first phone call from a potential client it is a good idea to compile a resource index. This can be anything from a small notebook to a computer data base, but its purpose is to enable you to make referrals when you cannot for some reason see a client yourself. There are several circumstances where this resource might be useful, for example, clients may contact you, but then realise that the journey to your consulting room would be too far. They may not be able to manage the hours which you are offering. You may have personal reasons why you are unable to work with a particular client, for example choosing not to work with issues of bereavement immediately after a personal loss. Clients may need specialist help outside what you offer, such as a group for alcoholics or a specialist adviser for a particular problem.

Your list should include local as well as specialist services further afield. Useful resources include The British Association for Counselling *Counselling and Psychotherapy Resources Directory* and the lists of practitioners published by other professional psychotherapy and counselling organisations. Your Citizens Advice Bureau may be able to help with local suggestions.

As well as practitioners, include the following in your index showing names, addresses, phone numbers, qualifications, services and specialisations offered:

- Statutory services (e.g. psychiatric, housing and social services).
- Practitioners offering a different service (e.g. couple counselling, groupwork or family therapy).
- Practitioners offering a different style of work (e.g. psychodynamic, cognitive, behavioural).
- Practitioners offering a different kind of therapy (e.g. aromatherapy, hypnosis or massage).
- Other supportive services (e.g. helplines).
- Accident and emergency departments.
- Police.
- 24-hour lawyers.

Size of workload

How many clients will you be seeing each day? Ask yourself what your ideal balance would be. You may well feel unable to see seven or eight clients for fifty minutes each on every day of the week without becoming stressed and overloaded, so when planning your work and your income you need to build some space into your working day. Set aside non-client contact time for note writing, supervision, further training and relaxation (Wilkins, 1997). If you plan to work full time, try to fill your working week with a variety of tasks. If you intend to work part-time, then acknowledge that as well as counselling or psychotherapy sessions, your working hours should contain all the necessary support for client work. Do not be tempted to let it spill over into too many evenings, weekends, and other time off work. I once met a man who claimed to have thirty-five client contact hours each week, but he admitted that it was exhausting. No-one needs to work at that intensity; it is neither healthy for practitioners nor for their clients, and if you find yourself working that hard it is likely you are not charging enough or not marketing your business properly.

Your hours of work

Think ahead about whether you intend to work in the evenings or at the weekends rather than allow yourself to drift into doing so. Most clients who are prepared to pay private fees will be working during the day and will hope to see you in the evenings or possibly early mornings, but how will that fit in with your family and leisure time? Consider setting aside just one or two days each week when you are prepared to work unsocial hours rather than be pushed into it every day by client demands. You may lose some work this way, but you will feel resentful if you agree to appointment times that are not convenient to you and you are unlikely to work well with a client in these circumstances.

Philip, a priest, was encouraged by his bishop to divide his day into three segments, morning, afternoon and evening. Every day he set aside one segment for relaxation, and two for work, so if he had meetings to attend in the evening he took the afternoon or morning off.

Working for yourself can bring with it a sense that you have to keep earning money, but you should not do this at the expense of a balanced existence. Consider early morning appointments or lunchtimes for people who work locally. In reality a lunch hour can be anything from 11.30am to 3.30pm which represents quite a large slice of the working day. Don't be tempted to fit your life entirely around the needs of your clients. This is an easy mistake to make in the early days when you are keen to take on as many clients as you can manage. Depending on the competition in your locality, the quality of your service and the prices you charge, you may be able to impose a higher fee for clients who you see during unsocial hours, or better still budget your fees so that you offer a reduction for people who are able to come during the normal working day.

Working people will be well placed to pay a full fee but those on benefit will not. While the latter group will have less income they will probably be more flexible about the times they can come for sessions. Consider offering reduced fee sessions at those times of day when there is less demand.

A growing number of employers offer a flexitime arrangement which allows people time off provided they make up their hours later. Some understanding employers will even allow time off for a member of staff who is undergoing counselling or psycho-therapy, especially if they are likely to become a more productive employee as a result. If you find that lunchtimes and early evening sessions are in demand, remember that working clients tend to fall into three categories, namely those who will take time off from work to attend sessions (without telling their boss), those who are supported by their employer and given time off to attend and those who come resentfully and simply because they feel it is expected of them. The final category are rarely committed to working well. Either they resent being sent to see you or they are angry with their employers and keen to attend just to run up bills which their employer will have to pay. However, you should never assume that because someone is in work they are unable to attend during the normal working day.

While on the subject of resentful clients you should also be prepared for those who tell you, 'I have to go into therapy because it is a condition of the counselling course I'm on.' Unless they are prepared to own their need to develop their self-awareness it is unlikely that they will benefit from seeing you.

Counselling or psychotherapy by nature should be a containing experience, and this applies as much to the appointment times as to the emotional containment you offer clients during their sessions. Set times made available for appointments can test a client's motivation for change in their lives. If they are prepared to negotiate time off work, arrange child care or temporarily give up sporting or social activities this may involve considerable personal or financial sacrifice on their part, and this should be recognised. However, practitioners who are regularly prepared to work at any time (day, night, weekends, early mornings, Sundays and bank holidays) may not be adequately looking after their own needs.

The behaviour of clients who have a problem with keeping appointments should be open to challenge and interpretation but there are people who have a genuine difficulty with regular hours. A senior company director protested that only the most awkward time slots were available from his therapist, but recognised that it was worth re-arranging his life to fit in sessions if it would improve his marriage. A nurse who worked shifts had genuine difficulty fitting into an appointment system that demanded attendance at the same time every week, so her counsellor agreed to make an exception and offer fortnightly sessions. Consider how flexible you would be if approached by someone whose work, family, health or caring responsibilities meant that they could not make appointments within the normal service you offer. Making a blunt psychodynamic interpretation of resistance and avoidance may not always be appropriate and will simply drive some clients away.

Many practitioners work to the 'fifty minute hour'. A ten minute break between clients to write notes and to adjust to the next person's needs has traditionally enabled practitioners to offer appointments on the hour. Charging a client say £25 a session is the equivalent of a meter ticking away at 50p a minute (more expensive incidentally than some premium rate telephone chat lines). Consequently, many clients are simply unable to afford a full fifty minute session. A request for monthly or fortnightly sessions rather than weekly ones if explored may reveal a lack of time or too many other commitments. But it is well worth listening carefully to what clients are saying. What is the real objection, is it lack of money, time or motivation, or is it your personality, style of work or even your premises that your clients object to? For example, it is much easier for a client to say 'I'll think about it' and then not come back again, than to say 'I'm scared to walk down your street at night so I'm not coming again.'

Where money is a real issue for the client, the choice you offer does not have to be simply between providing a full fifty minute session at full cost or no session at all. It may be possible to offer shorter sessions for half or three-quarters of your normal fee. This unusual arrangement is nevertheless a pragmatic one. There are other options too. One practitioner travels to see her supervisor one morning a fortnight and keeps the alternate weekly time free for short-term, low-fee paying clients. Another has an arrangement to refer clients who are unable to pay private fees to a local charitable counselling centre. In return she provides a couple of free sessions each week.

Other options for work

If you are successful in your practice this may reduce your levels of stress but if not it may increase them. So before you commit yourself to a full-time private practice, ask yourself if there are any other ways in which you could gain more control over your daily life. You might for instance hope to work three days a week seeing private clients and act as a consultant for an employer or work within a GP practice on the other two. Or, you might consider working part-time or through an agency where you can choose the hours you work. If you are moving from employment to self-employment you may simply be exchanging one set of problems for another. You may lose out on employment benefits such as holiday and sickness pay, pension contributions and health insurance schemes and so you will need to weigh this up against the greater control you will have over your time.

Health

Think carefully about how your business would survive economically if you were ill:

Alan had a successful private practice as a counsellor but after a few years contracted hepatitis. He had a lengthy period of time off sick. Fortunately he was able to live with his parents as he recovered but his business collapsed. He had no medical insurance and had to start up all over again. Not only did he lose his existing clients, but he was left with debts for the long-term lease he had taken out on his consulting room.

Sickness benefit is very small, and no real help when it comes to a protracted illness or hospital stay. Consider whether to subscribe to an insurance scheme, or to rely on capital and savings or family support in the event of a health problem. Recurrent illness makes counselling or psychotherapy a poor choice as a profession since you need to be fit to generate regular income and your clients need you to be reliable. If your health is unpredictable, this is another factor to take into account before deciding to work in private practice (Daines et al., 1997).

Once part-time working and self-employment were seen as secondary to gaining a permanent job. Nowadays however, there is a growing tendency for employees only to be offered part-time or temporary contracts and this means a corresponding growth in the attraction of self-employment. Having personal control over expansion or contraction of the work may be attractive to those who have other part-time work which is not sufficient or not entirely reliable as an income. It may also appeal to those who have child care responsibilities or other caring roles.

Training

Before embarking on a career in private practice you should consider whether the level of training that you have received has equipped you for this. For example, how would you cope with a client who was suffering from serious mental health problems? Would you be able to assess whether your client was suffering from a psychotic or disordered state of mind, and would you recognise your own need to refer the client to a psychiatrist for an independent assessment? (Daines et al., 1997; Palmer and McMahon, 1997). Some people who have undertaken very basic training in counselling skills may erroneously believe that this sets them up to work privately which is both unethical and potentially damaging for clients. The British Association for Counselling has acknowledged this problem by publishing two separate Codes of Ethics, one for people who use counselling skills in the course of their work such as teachers, nurses and social workers and another for those who view themselves as professional practitioners engaged in counselling as the main aspect of their work.

Although efforts are being made to standardise the quality of counselling and psychotherapy training, there is a wide range of courses available including some that offer very basic training with no client contact at all. Even correspondence courses are available in counselling where students rarely see a lecturer let alone a client. Courses with a high academic content do not necessarily provide practical, supervised experience of client work as part of their training package. However, a period of supervised counselling or psychotherapy practice in an organisational setting is essential before seeing clients in private practice. Many people do obtain this experience as part of their training and there are certainly benefits in undergoing theoretical and practical training simultaneously. However, work or family commitments for some or a gradually emerging sense of career direction for others may make this impractical. Students sometimes achieve experience by providing assessments at a voluntary counselling centre in exchange for free supervision; undergoing an honorary psychotherapy placement at a psychiatric hospital, or providing counselling sessions for a mental health charity. Some will be able to undertake client work as an extension of their existing career. What is important is that you complete a period of practical, supervised therapeutic activity, probably a minimum of 100 hours before starting a private practice. If it is your intention to see clients as a full time occupation, then considerably more experience would be advisable.

There are several professional bodies who will give advice on whether the training you have undertaken equips you for private practice. The United Kingdom Council for Psychotherapy (UKCP), the British Association for Counselling, the British Psychological Society (BPS) or the British Confederation of Psychotherapists (BCP) will assist. Seek the views of your own training institution as they may be able to offer additional training for people entering private practice.

Working to a Code of Ethics and Practice

Your training institution may already have agreed a Code of Ethics and Practice to which you subscribe. If it has not, it is in your interests to subscribe to a recognised counselling or psychother-apy professional body which does have one. If you are in doubt, speak to the British Association for Counselling. Such a Code should protect the interests of you and your clients in the case of any future conflict, providing a clear statement of how you work, setting out what clients can and cannot expect from you and providing guidance to them on how any future complaint against you would be independently investigated. A Code of Ethics helps to protect clients from unscrupulous practitioners, but it is also a protection for practitioners. Remember that quite apart from those few clients who have genuine grievances, there will always be some who will follow the complaints route or even take legal action as a means of dealing with their anger. The issue may be relatively trivial or relate to emotions and behaviour that has not been effectively interpreted. Great care needs to be taken when handling such people. Consult Bond (1993) and Syme (1994) for further clarification of specifically ethical matters.

Complaints

Objective investigation of complaints can only be carried out by an impartial third party. Some professional bodies are better equipped than others when it comes to carrying out this important work. An independent person who is familiar with the working style of the practitioner but not known personally to him or her should be appointed by the body to investigate.

Most professional bodies report some complaints against their members each year and can offer a range of remedies such as ordering a practitioner to attend additional supervision or even expulsion from their professional body. It could be argued that expulsion should only be the last resort as it is normally better to keep an errant practitioner within an organisation that may be able to offer guidance, support or re-training.

As membership of such a body is not currently a legal requirement in order to practise in the UK, this sanction has no real teeth other than professional embarrassment. This is a matter which will surely be addressed when and if the whole profession becomes subject to regulation by statute as the ability to continue practising contrasts strongly with the power of the British Medical Association to 'strike off' medical practitioners.

One practitioner reports that their professional body actually made matters worse by mishandling an initial investigation and making erroneous statements to the client who subsequently used these misleading statements against him to threaten legal action. Be certain that any investigation will be full and fair to you as well as to your client before agreeing to take part. Sometimes it might be preferable to say nothing, play no part in the investigations and simply wait for the client to sue for damages. In that way they will need to prove their case against you. See Jenkins (1997) for further details on complaints procedures and legal issues.

Insurance

Anyone in private practice, whatever the quality of their work, may find themselves being sued by a client claiming that damage has been done to them. It is not only unethical practitioners who get embroiled in accusations of malpractice so it is essential to be insured. It is not expensive, but legal bills can be, so you should consider cover of up to one or two million pounds in case a client does sue you for professional malpractice. Your professional body may have arranged a discounted insurance scheme for its members, covering public liability as well as professional indemnity for your work. From time to time this type of work will inevitably bring you into contact with people who have severe mental health problems. Some may want to blame you for their ills, others may go so far as legal action. Should you find yourself in this situation you should immediately inform your insurers.

Chapter summary

- For success, all businesses need careful planning. Have you considered how much investment of a financial and a personal nature you will need to put into your business?
- How will a private practice mix with the kind of life you lead? What will the effects be on your relationships, your family, your time and your income and how will these in turn affect your practice?
- Why do you want to work for yourself? What draws you to this kind of work? Why do you regard it as being an improvement on working for an organisation?
- Are you sufficiently self-motivated to put energy into your own business, to strive for success and to stick it out when there is a challenge to overcome? Would you feel more comfortable working for someone else or letting others take responsibility for the business?
- Are you fit enough to assume that you will regularly be available for work?
- Has your training to date sufficiently equipped you for working in a counselling or psychotherapy private practice and not simply taught you basic counselling skills for use elsewhere?
- Do you have the backing of a supervisor who knows your work, and agrees that you are capable of working privately?
- Have you been a client yourself in personal therapy during your training and are you planning to continue or prepared to enter into a new personal therapy relationship should the need arise?
- Have you made arrangements for consultation as necessary with a psychiatrist who has access to hospital beds and medication?
- Do you have a resource index so that you can make appropriate referrals?
- Are you signed up to a well publicised and nationally recognised Code of Ethics which protects you and your clients and offers access to a complaints procedure?
- Are you covered by professional indemnity insurance?

2

Business and Private Practice

Finance

Getting the money side of your business right from the start is essential for more businesses fail for lack of financial planning than for any other reason. If you follow the step-by-step approach in this chapter you will be able to plan realistically for a successful practice. There are five key stages, these are:

- A Personal Budget (your own requirements for income).
- A Business Plan (what you hope your practice will achieve).
- A Practice Income Budget (what you anticipate your business income will be).
- A Practice Expenditure Budget (what you anticipate your costs will be).
- Cashflow (making certain you have enough money available at any one time).

You cannot expect to be an expert at every aspect of running a business, so there will be times when you will need to use the services of professional advisers such as solicitors or accountants. Unless you have some knowledge of how to market your service and keep your books yourself, you will need to pay someone else to do these things for you. If in doubt about any of these matters you should always seek professional advice. An accountant's fees will be based on the amount of work they do for you, so decide early on which aspects of bookkeeping you can cover for yourself and which require specialist help. Keeping clear accounts from the beginning will cost you less than if you rely entirely on your accountant.

Your personal budget

How much personal income do you need? Few people plan in detail the amount of money they need to earn. We might dream about winning the lottery or have a rough idea about the money we need to pay our bills, but for most people our lives are a complicated mixture of relative successes and failures, of disappointments and surprises. Career moves sometimes pay off with promotion and more responsibility but can result in a dead-end job with no prospects or redundancy. Becoming self-employed in any profession means you will be fully responsible for developing and maintaining income, so you will need to have a clear idea about your limits of relative success or failure.

When working out your current requirements for income you should remember that bills arrive at different times. Some, like motor insurance and holidays, may arrive once a year, mortgage repayments and life assurance will be payable monthly, and you will need to eat every day no matter how often you go shopping. Items like council tax can be paid annually, half-yearly or even over ten months and while school dinner money may have to be found in cash each week, children still have to be fed in the school holidays! Adjust the figures so that you come out with an average cost for everything you spend throughout the year. Make certain you use monthly or weekly figures consistently throughout. Remember that items of expenditure may be paid for by bank account, credit card or cash. Divide them between the headings of home, family, transport and borrowing. Everything should fit into one of these main categories.

Most of us tend to underestimate our expenses and over-estimate our income, partly because we do not usually keep a detailed account of our cash expenses. So you should not rush this process. Try keeping a notebook on you and recording every single cash transaction, however small, for a whole month. Relatively small cash items such as stamps, chocolates, newspapers and parking meters can eat into your budget surprisingly quickly.

Table 2.1   *Private monthly expenditure budget*

Home	(£)
Mortgage or rent	350
Life assurance	65
Mortgage protection insurance	20
Home maintenance	50
Council tax	60
Gas	30
Electricity	40
Water and sewerage	18
Home telephone	22
TV licence/rental cable/satellite	32
Food shopping	400
Take aways	40
Meals out	50
Newspapers/magazines	8
Laundry/dry cleaning	10
School dinners	30
School trips	15
Clothes adults	60
Clothes children	40
Personal requisites	15
Holidays away	100
Days out	20
Christmas/festivals	30
Birthdays	30
Confectionery	5
Alcohol	20
Clubs/subscriptions	10
Charity donations	10
Adult personal spending allowance	80
Children's pocket money	40
Savings account	60
Train, bus and taxi fares	20
Season ticket or loan	120
Car/motorcycle tax	12
Car/motorcycle insurance	24
MOT	3
Servicing	30
Petrol and oil	60
Parking	6
Breakdown membership	5
Allowance for vehicle depreciation	60
Total monthly expenditure	2,100

For the purpose of the examples in this chapter, meet Paul. He is a 40-year-old social work consultant. He has two children at primary school and a mortgage and his expenditure budget can be seen in Table 2.1.

Multiplying this figure of £2,100 by twelve Paul calculated the minimum annual income he required, after tax and other deductions, was £25,200. Now make a similar calculation of your own needs using the Financial Plan in Appendix 1. When you are confident that you have an accurate assessment, write it all down and it will look something like Paul's calculations. Take time over this, remembering that the total will be the minimum amount you will need to live on in order to maintain your existing standard of living. It is also the net amount, that is to say the amount you need after the deduction of your business expenses and your income tax and national insurance contributions. Remember to include any items that apply to you but not to Paul. For example becoming self-employed will probably mean making payments into a private pension scheme.

Once you have done this, try re-working your example, with different figures. How would your needs differ if you decided to take out a loan repayable at £150 a month to buy a car, or if you halved the amount you currently saved? Do you need a car at all or could you manage on public transport? You might decide to send your children to a fee paying school but spend less on meals out and holidays. Would you be prepared to forgo a holiday altogether for the first year or two while your practice was being established? By how much will the picture change when your children are grown up, if your partner decides to change jobs or an elderly relative becomes in need of support? Gradually you will develop a clear picture of what proportion of your income is absolutely essential and what is simply desirable. The aim is to have a clear idea of the absolute minimum income you need on which to live.

Your business budget

Once you have a reasonably clear idea of your own financial needs you can then start work on a business budget for your practice. You will need to do some research to estimate the income and expenditure that it is likely to produce.

Paul had undertaken some evening classes in counselling skills and managed to set aside a day each week to attend a course offering a diploma in counselling practice. He assisted at a youth club one night each week where he already used some counselling skills and wanted to develop this into a career.

Before drawing up his plans in detail he thought about spreading the costs as far as possible throughout the year. For example, if he rented premises payments would fall due each quarter but he would have some control over the months in which he paid for advertising and promotion. These costs could be adjusted to fit with the growth of his practice. In this way, as far as possible, he would not have to meet very high bills one month and substantially reduced ones the next. These are the main items of expenditure he expected to encounter.

Rent

Local estate agents (some will have a commercial section) are able to advise on the cost of renting office accommodation. In many areas licensed accommodation is also available where all bills including rates and electricity and sometimes even telephone, fax and secretarial services are included in a single monthly payment. Renting a consulting room is the largest single cost for most practitioners, so many people choose to work from home. Because this makes a considerable difference to costs, the examples have been drawn up to show these options separately (see Tables 2.2 and 2.3).

Table 2.2 *Business plan – expenses budget (with a home-based consulting room)*

Item	First quarter	Second quarter	Third quarter	Final quarter	Annual totals
Contribution to bills	30	30	30	30	120
Phone	60	60	60	60	240
Supervision	240	240	240	240	960
Travel	50	50	50	50	200
Print/advertising	300				300
Professional fees		60	60		120
Bank charges	20	20	20	20	80
Totals	700	460	460	400	2020

Table 2.3 *Business plan – expenses (with a separate consulting room)*

Item	First quarter	Second quarter	Third quarter	Final quarter	Annual totals
Rent	600	600	600	600	2400
Rates		120		120	240
Water		60		60	120
Heat/light	30	30	30	30	120
Phone	60	60	60	60	240 ·
Supervision	240	240	240	240	960
Travel	400	400	400	400	1600
Print/advertising	500				500
Professional fees		60	60		120
Bank charges	20	20	20	20	80
Totals	1850	1590	1410	1530	6380

Business rates
This is payable on business premises, council tax is payable on private dwellings (see Chapter 5).

Utilities
Your heating, lighting and telephone bills will of course depend on usage and size of rooms. You can work out roughly what to expect from your domestic bills but higher levels of VAT may apply to energy supplied to a business. If you work from home you may be able to allocate some of your domestic bills to your business.

Supervision
This is cited by many practitioners as the single most expensive item after premises, nevertheless it is an essential cost.

Travel
If your practice is based in premises outside your home, you will need to budget for travelling to and from work. You should note that if you travel to one regular place of work, you will probably not be able to offset the cost of this travel against your income tax. If you visit clients, or do consultancy work for other organisations you should however be able to offset this. The cost of travelling to supervision and other relevant business meetings or

conferences should also be included. Your local Inland Revenue office will explain the rules in detail.

Printing stationery and advertising

All new businesses need a budget for advertising or at the very least producing leaflets, contracts, invoices and business cards. It will add to your image as a professional if your stationery is well designed and produced. Obtain quotations from local printers. Alternatively, if you have access to a computer with desktop publishing facilities you may be able to do the work yourself. Quality of colour print on home publishing systems has improved considerably in recent years so explore all options before spending large sums of money at the printers.

Professional fees

Include your annual subscriptions to professional bodies which support you in your work for example through accreditation, registration or continuing professional development as well as the fees paid to your accountant, solicitor and so on.

Bank charges

Business accounts are normally subject to higher bank charges than personal accounts. Think whether you really require one if your accounts are simple.

Having explored these budget headings and made reasonable estimates of what each one might cost him in a year, Paul estimated that his business costs would look like those in Table 2.2 if he worked from home and like Table 2.3 if he rented a consulting room.

Clearly, there is a considerable difference between the two total costs estimates of £2,020 and £6,380. Consequently the decision whether to work from home or a separate consulting room may be crucial for the success of the practice, especially in the early days.

Estimating income was however much more difficult for Paul. How could he be sure of getting any clients at all? There seemed to be a demand for counselling locally where not many people were offering a service. He checked the average fees that were charged by people in his county. He did this by reference to the British Association for Counselling *Directory of Counselling and*

Table 2.4 *Business plan – working days*

Month	First quarter	Second quarter	Third quarter	Final quarter	Annual totals
Calendar days	90	91	92	92	365
Working Days	65	65	65	70	265
(Less Holidays	1	9	20	7	37)
(Less Sickness				5	5)
Total working days	64	56	45	58	223

Psychotherapy. He knew from his own therapy that some practitioners were prepared to negotiate so assumed that the true market rate was slightly less than people were actually seeking. What level of fees would ensure regular business and yet cover his costs and help him remain competitive?

Paul planned to see a minimum of five clients each day paying £25 per each. He recognised that there were sometimes four and sometimes five weeks in each month and that there were eight bank holidays when he would not be working. His health was good but as a precaution he would allow for one week off work in the year for illness. He planned to charge clients if they missed a session but would not charge clients while he was on holiday himself. He would be away for all of August and take a week off at Christmas and Easter. He planned to set aside two evenings a week to see clients in the first year as this would make his service flexible and would gradually reduce his other work as his practice expanded. Next Paul drew up another chart (Table 2.4) to calculate the actual time that he would have available for work in the coming year.

Paul then decided that his target income for the first year would be as follows:

A minimum of five daily individual sessions at £25 each for 223 days	27,875
An employee consultancy to a local major employer	4,675
Six workshops charged at £400	2,400
Three terms of evening class lecturing at £500 a term	1,500
Sub-total	36,450
Less expenses first year working from home	2,020
Total	34,430

Try running a similar prediction for your own business income. Look over Paul's figures once again before you write your own up. Yours will need to be based on local market conditions so do some local research. Remember fees vary considerably across the country, averaging between £15 and £30 an hour but with many people charging much more than this and some charging less.

Cashflow

Before embarking on any major project from home decorating to holidays, it is sensible to be clear about how much it will cost. The same is true of starting a business. You may guess that you can see, say twelve clients each week, paying £20 each, but this does not of course mean that you will have £240 a week to spend how you like. From this money you will need to find all your business expenses, your tax and national insurance contributions and your profits from which you will pay yourself a wage. Many people fail to budget accurately for the expenses of their new business which are often particularly high in the first year because of the costs of setting up a business. You will therefore need to consider how your bills, both personal and business ones will be paid in those early days.

So once you have a reasonably clear idea of how much income and expenditure you are likely to incur, you should turn your thoughts to the timing of your receipts and bills. This is your cashflow and it is important because it will show you the amount of money you need to have at your disposal at any one time.

Planning on a rolling basis for the next twelve or eighteen months is a good idea at this stage and you can soon begin to forecast trading patterns based on actual business experience. This will help you clarify with your bank manager whether you need an overdraft facility. To think about this in a realistic way you will need to draw up a cash flow chart like the one below. In Paul's case his business income was planned at £36,450 in the first year. Profit is lower at £34,430 because expenditure of £2,020 has been deducted. Not everyone will achieve an income like this. Some will do even better while others will not even achieve this degree of success. This will depend on many factors including motivation, marketing, pricing and commitment to seeing clients at times they can manage.

Table 2.5   *Business plan – income and cashflow*

	First quarter	Second quarter	Third quarter	Final quarter	Year end
Income					
Clients	4,646	9,892	5,146	8,191	27,875
Consultancy	1,169	1,169	1,169	1,168	4,675
Workshops	600	600	600	600	2,400
Lecturing		500	500	500	1,500
Sub-totals	6,415	12,161	7,415	10,459	36,450
Less expenses	700	460	460	400	2,020
Profit	5,715	11,701	6,955	10,059	34,430

Paul checked the potential income from his practice against his costs in the first year, the results of this can be seen in Table 2.5.

Inevitably some expenses will be necessary before you start seeing your clients. Even working from home you will need to publicise your service, provide comfortable furnishings, fit an answering machine and maybe a separate phone line. You may decide to redecorate. If you choose to use premises outside your home, you will probably need to pay a deposit and advance rental payments, on top of the basic furniture, stationery and telephone requirements. Can you fund this out of your savings or from personal or family capital? If you can get an interest free borrowing arranged, perhaps by borrowing from relatives, that may be the best way to fund a business; if not a trip to the bank manager will be required.

A business bank account

Now is the time to get your bank account sorted out. Banks offer advice, and all the major ones offer plenty on the topic of how to start a new business. They want your custom and it is in their interest as much as yours to help you off to a successful start. Their literature includes advice on how to draw up a business plan and predict your income and expenditure. Before you tell the bank that you are going to be running a business, check what the different charges are for a personal account and a self-employed business account. Most banks will offer free banking to small businesses in the first year of operation, but don't be tempted by this. Consider the fact that a small private practice will generate fewer transactions than some personal accounts, especially in the first year. If you are a sole trader open another account so that you keep your business income and expenditure separate from your personal money and a savings account to set aside your income tax and national insurance contributions. Doing this will help you with your bookkeeping when you come to agree your books. However as soon as you declare it as a business account you may pay charges, probably for every item that goes through your account. There are plenty of banks and building societies to choose from so if they want to charge you should go elsewhere.

Presenting your plans

Bank managers want to hear sensible proposals, so if you plan to borrow you will need to be realistic. Discussing your plans with an accountant first will be helpful, and you will probably need an accountant once your business is operating anyway. Be ready to show that you have researched your market carefully and that you can demonstrate a sound knowledge of the business you are undertaking. Bank managers are more likely to be sympathetic if you have already tested the market, perhaps by working success-fully from home or for an agency that is growing and guaranteeing to make referrals to you. Alternatively they will want to know about the plans you have to market and develop your practice.

Your cash flow predictions are the key to a successful applica-tion for borrowing. Be clear about the amount you need and the period for which you may require it. Be honest about any doubts you have before finalising your calculation. For example, what action will you be taking if you fail to attract as many clients as you had hoped for or clients finish and leave faster than you had expected? How will you ensure that your clients pay you regu-larly? If you agree to weekly payment and you later allow them to stretch out to monthly payments, this will adversely affect your cashflow.

Banks usually charge an arrangement fee for an overdraft and at each annual review. Even if you have a long relationship with your own bank, you should shop around because you may find better terms elsewhere. Some direct (telephone) banking services do not have the cost of maintaining a branch network, and Scottish banks are keen to obtain English or Welsh business and so may offer better terms than the well known English high street banks. Treat banks just like supermarkets or estate agents, don't be tempted by the first offer and be prepared to compare offers.

Remember that banks are there to make a profit for their shareholders, not just as a resource for the community. They can only do this by lending money to good risk businesses. So if they turn you down, you should not blame your bank manager. Try elsewhere by all means, but reflect carefully on any suggestions that are made to you. Every year, about half of all new businesses fail, often because they have not had sufficient capital to survive the first year. Your bank manager may have some sound advice for you and even if it means delaying or changing your plans, think carefully about what is being said.

Offering security

Be careful with what you sign because banks usually require security for a substantial business loan and although this reduces their risks (and consequently the level of interest rate that they charge you), you should not allow your home or anything else of value to be used as security unless you are prepared to risk losing it. Determine the relative benefits of a loan or overdraft to develop your business. For most people their home is their greatest asset and so a mortgage or business loan secured against the home is not something to be undertaken lightly. You would need to discuss such a proposal with your spouse, partner or anyone who has a joint interest in the property.

Overdrafts

Unlike a retail business where profit is made from continuously buying goods and selling them at a profit, a counselling or psychotherapy practice is a service based business, with only your time and skills for sale. Consequently, once you have covered your major costs (such as supervision, rent and telephone charges) you will have little further expenditure however many clients you see and this means that you are less likely (than say a greengrocer) to need an overdraft once your business is well established.

An overdraft facility of say £2,000 or so might be handy, perhaps to see you through setting up costs or cover the summer holiday period when you are not working. However you should never use an overdraft as a substitute for planned income. Be clear where the money to repay it will come from and whether the money you borrow really is for the benefit of the business or for your own personal needs. For some purchases you may find it cheaper to use a bank credit card with an interest free period which may give you up to almost eight weeks interest free credit.

Renting premises

Consider the costs you are likely to incur in the course of establishing a small practice and operating it for the first year. If you rent a room for consultations, this is likely to be the most significant expense that you will have. For this reason many people decide to work from home initially, at least until they are clear about how much income they can generate. Later on when the business has developed this can be a good time to decide to use premises outside the home. Additional costs will be incurred but there may be other factors to consider such as the demands of a growing family, insufficient workspace or lack of privacy for clients or family.

On current prices you could expect to pay suburban office rental of least £8 to £15 per square foot per annum, depending on quality, so even a small 12' by 15' room would cost over £100 each month. You would pay far more for Central London or convenient locations in other major cities. Sharing with another practitioner could ensure the room is fully utilised from the beginning but would need careful planning to avoid difficulties.

Adrian, Margaret and Jack were a psychotherapist, aroma-therapist and acupuncturist respectively. They agreed to share premises on the understanding that they would not form a business partnership as such, but simply share the rental of the building between them. With the help of a solicitor they drew up an agreement which defined the cost to each of them and made clear which days and times they could have exclusive use of the premises. This way they were able to market and develop their own practices separately

but combine for mutually beneficial activity such as pub-
licity and the referral of clients to one another.

Supervision as a cost

New practitioners may often pay more for their supervision than
they charge their own clients for sessions, perhaps feeling that a
higher price signifies experience and competence. But this is not
always the case. Discussions with practitioners produced some
surprising results. Some were paying extremely high fees for
supervision which appeared to be of an equal quality to that
provided by supervisors charging a much lower fee. Others with
equally competent supervisors were simply making donations to a
charity which employed the supervisor.

The cost of supervision is sometimes wrongly used as an
argument against using a supervisor at all, especially when starting out:

Clarke decided to see a couple of clients at home each
week during his training. As he was a student he felt only
able to charge them £10 each. Quotes he obtained for
weekly supervision ranged upwards from £30. Unethically
and despite the advice of his lecturers he decided to manage
without supervision altogether. His logic was that this
would avoid running his practice at a loss. He thought it
unlikely that he would do any damage to his clients, but
within a month both of them were dissatisfied and left. Had
he been in supervision he would at least have had the
opportunity to reflect on his work and this would probably
have helped him work more effectively.

Supervision should be viewed as a fixed and continuous cost
throughout the life of your practice. It is as much of an investment
in your business as the practical tools you have such as furniture
and an answering machine. Those who are starting out in private
practice with just one or two clients may be tempted to manage
without supervision but quite apart from being unethical this is a
poor business decision to make. If you are in this position ask
yourself whether you have the long term aim of operating an
expanding and successful practice or whether you are simply
testing it out as a possible career. Your practice will need financial

as well as professional commitment and if you cannot afford supervision from day one you should seriously reconsider whether this work is right for you.

Supervision fees remain a regular cost to the business for the length of your practice so it is important to agree a realistic and sustainable price. You should negotiate the cost of supervision as you would for personal therapy and be prepared to find several quotes. You may not require sessions as frequently as weekly (although these can be very useful when first starting up) but you will be offering your supervisor commited and regular business.

Supervisors find professional stimulation working with a supervisee who has a professional approach. This is particularly so when a supervisee is prepared to reflect constructively on their work. Most supervisors probably see clients as well, but value the additional stimulation which supervision brings. It is interesting work, bringing with it regular income and affirmation to the supervisor that they have achieved a certain level of experience and training themselves.

There are other costs involved in supervision. Before committing yourself consider the distance and travelling costs involved and the time and frequency of your meetings which might prevent you from taking on specific pieces of work. For most practitioners this will become one of the highest costs of their business, second only to outlay on premises, so it is as well to keep it closely under control.

You will want to be clear about the terms under which your supervisor works. Unlike a client coming for therapy, there should be no need for you to pay for holiday time, sickness or other missed appointments, and it would be helpful to know that on occasions you could have prompt access by phone to discuss a case in between sessions. As when seeking personal therapy for yourself you should define your requirements carefully in advance and be prepared to shop around for choice and value.

Setting a client fee structure

The price of any goods or services depends on two factors, namely supply and demand. It follows therefore that the cost of providing a service to clients and the local demand for counselling or psychotherapy are what will determine the fees that you are able to charge.

In rural areas, practitioners are few and far between and lower population levels means the demand for services is relatively low. Additional time spent travelling may make it more difficult for some clients to book regular appointments and this in turn reduces demand. Conversely some of the London and other major city practitioners listed in the BAC Counselling and Psychotherapy Resources Directory seek to charge the highest fees in the country, justifying this because they have the greater living and commercial costs to sustain. They are likely to have a more regular flow of business partly because more people live or work in cities and partly because it is generally accepted that city life tends to be more stressful than in the countryside. However, different kinds of stresses bring people to counselling wherever they live. Isolation and depression can be just as real whether caused by living in a tower block or an isolated farmhouse.

Research carefully what fees are being charged by the counsellors and psychotherapists in your area. Current evidence suggests that practitioners in urban areas seek between £25 and £35 per session but frequently have to settle for something nearer £20. Those more isolated may need to accept something nearer £15. Some practitioners offer a sliding scale of fees. Some negotiate according to each client's ability to pay, others publish a scale based upon the client's net income. With any of these approaches it is necessary to have a regular supply of full-fee paying clients to subsidise others. This is an area where some practitioners have difficulty because of their conflicts between being businesslike and compassionate. Those who have been used to public service employment may fail to recognise that if fees do not cover costs then their business will eventually fail.

Having set your fee rates keep them under review at least annually. It is better to charge increased fees to new clients as you take them on rather than raise fees for existing clients unless you have worked with them for a considerable period of time, say two years or more. Frequent increases simply give the impression that your business is poorly managed and does nothing to enhance your reputation. This is another argument for carefully pitching your fees at the right level from the start.

Chapter summary

- How much income do you need?
- Where will it come from while you establish your business?
- What alternatives do you have if you do not achieve your target income?
- Write a business plan before you start to see clients.
- How much will it all cost and will you need to borrow money?
- Open a separate bank account for your business.
- How will you set and review client fees?

3

Trading Style, Accounts, Taxes and Private Practice

Trading style

Before you start up in business you will need to make a choice about your trading style, that is the way in which your business is legally structured. Like all businesses you will have a choice of three styles which are self-employment, partnerships or limited company. There is actually a fourth trading style known as public companies (the ones that have 'plc' after their names and are listed on the Stock Exchange) but that need not worry us here.

If you are setting up a small private practice you will probably want to start by adopting a self-employed status. This is the most straightforward way of trading, for all you need to do is fill in a simple form to register your self-employed status with the Department of Social Security (DSS) office. Their local office will be found in your telephone book. You will have to pay a regular monthly contribution to them to cover state sickness benefit and pension contributions. The easiest way to do this is by direct debit. This way even if the DSS made a mistake and overcharged you, you would be able to get an immediate refund from your bank.

A self-employed person is held to be available for work (even if they have no clients and no income) so they are not entitled to unemployment benefit when times are lean. You become responsible for paying your own tax and national insurance contributions on the profits that your business makes and you will be billed every half year for the income tax and any additional national insurance payments based on your profits from the previous year's accounts.

Partnerships

If you plan to set up a business with a partner, you will need to consider how much of the business you each own, and therefore how you will split the profits. You may intend that you have equal shares, 50 per cent of the business each, or that one partner is a 'sleeping' partner, for example someone who puts up part of the money in return for say a 10 per cent share of the profits. Or they may provide a consulting room as their share of the costs, but not undertake any of the consultations. Even between friends and existing colleagues it is always important to be clear about how the profits from the practice are to be distributed and how many hours per week each will put into the business. If for example you open a joint bank account and run up an overdraft you will normally be 'jointly and severally liable' for the debt – this means that both or either of you could be pursued for the whole amount outstanding. It is of course important to have complete trust in a partner before going into business with them. Even if you feel confident about the arrangement now, circumstances can and do change and for this reason it is better to have a written agreement drawn up.

> *Simon and Mandy trained together as counsellors and decided to share a flat from which they would both offer counselling. This worked well for the first year, until Mandy met Eamon, got married and decided to stop practising as a counsellor. In addition to sorting out their joint tenancy of the flat, Simon and Mandy also had to call in an accountant and solicitor to help them clarify the share of the business profits which belonged to each of them.*

Limited companies

The third option is to consider setting up a limited company. This means that in law your business will be treated as if it is an individual in its own right. The advantage of this is that if your company fails leaving outstanding debts it will only be liable for an amount equivalent to the assets of the company. You as a director or shareholder will have what is known as 'limited liability', that is to say you will not be personally liable for your company's debts, unless you traded fraudulently or it could be demonstrated that you were grossly negligent in the operation of your business. This is an important level of protection and one that you do not have if you are self-employed or in a partnership. Against this you would need to balance the higher rate of tax, the additional paperwork and the annual returns that need to be made to Companies House. The main advantage however is that so long as you trade genuinely and not recklessly you may be able to take on liabilities such as bank loans, payments for a property lease and employment contracts without incurring personal liabilities if the business fails. Anyone can be the unfortunate victim of a business failure, but where company directors are shown to have deliberately set out to hoodwink their customers they can be barred from future directorships.

Keeping records

To be clear how much you are earning from your practice you will need to run a cash book. Unlike shops you will have relatively few daily transactions so book-keeping is relatively simple. Let's take one day as an example. You operate a sliding scale of fees according to income and you have a consultancy with a workplace counselling service as well as a supervisee that you see:

Client 1	One counselling session	£25
Client 2	One counselling session	£25
Supervisee	One supervision session	£40
Local company	Half-day consultancy	£120
Total day's income		£210

Next list your expenses. These are the items that you have incurred in the course of your business, say:

Supervision	£40
Stationery	£6
Fares to supervision	£8
Phone bill	£90
Total expenses	£144

From this starting point you can keep an eye on whether your business is making a profit or a loss. To provide a continuous view of whether you are making a profit or loss you will need to calculate cumulative figures, so each day you will need to add in the income and expenditure from previous days. Estimate these figures before you start your business and keep your estimates under review as the pattern of your business emerges. You will then be able to see at a glance whether you are generating enough income and containing your costs sufficiently.

Sometimes people choose to leave all this work to their accountants, but if they are not meeting at least weekly there is no guarantee that an accountant will pick up any problems in time. Whereas it is reasonably simple to keep fixed items such as rent and annual contracts under review, it is not so easy to keep a check on variable items such as short-term client fees and stationery costs. By the time the accountant gets to read the books of the business it may be too late to turn the business around, especially during the vital first few months. Some items such as telephone rental will be fixed costs, others such as advertising will be variable. Once your practice is well established you may feel able to monitor your accounts on just a quarterly basis.

Business mileage and travel costs

How much of your mileage can be counted as a justifiable business expense? The Inland Revenue will not allow you to claim travel to and from your normal place of work as a business expense. However, if you work in a number of locations, providing for example a consultancy service to various organisations you should be able to demonstrate that the costs of travel are a genuine business cost. If you simply leave home and drive to your consulting room each day then you will not be able to claim the cost of travel.

Other business costs

The finer points of what can and cannot be claimed as a genuine business expense depends upon established rules which your tax office or your accountant will explain. The basic rule is that each item needs to be an essential business expense and not simply one from which you derived personal benefit. You might successfully argue that magazines in a waiting room and fresh cut flowers in a consulting room were an essential part of providing a welcoming atmosphere for your clients. Supervision, personal indemnity insurance and fees to professional bodies are undoubtedly a necessary expense for most, but what about personal therapy? You might argue that therapy for yourself is an essential part of providing a service to your clients, on the other hand it could equally be argued by the tax authorities that you were deriving personal benefit from the therapy. If in doubt, claim what you can legally, any errors will be corrected by the Inland Revenue.

Value Added Tax

Value Added Tax (VAT) is collected by HM Government's Customs and Excise department and should not be confused with income tax. Early on when planning a business it is important to be clear whether that business is likely to exceed the current turnover limit for VAT registration (in 1997 £48,000 per annum). While that figure might seem a long way off in the early days, failing to be prepared for it when the time comes, can lead to serious penalties. If your turnover is approaching £4,000 a month then you should certainly be considering registration.

You can choose to register for VAT before you reach the registration figure and it would be prudent to do so in the year in which you start to approach the figure. Your accountant should give you advice on this. However, you would then need to levy a VAT charge on every invoice you issue. This means your clients would all need to pay VAT on top of their fees (currently at 17.5 per cent). Before handing this over to Customs and Excise, you would then be able to set against this the VAT that you had paid in the course of your business on items such as stationery and office equipment. Counselling and psychotherapy are labour intensive activities, with most of the income arriving from direct service provision and relatively little need for the purchase of goods or services. In that sense there is little 'added value' in the technical sense and therefore you are unlikely to pay out large amounts of VAT in the course of your work. However, this might be different were you to purchase a large item such as computer system or vehicle for the purpose of business travel. Unless you are rapidly approaching the registration limit you are likely to save yourself a lot of additional work by not registering, but it is important to monitor your situation carefully and an accountant should help you with this.

Income tax

Once you are registered as a self- employed person you will be allocated a tax reference by your district office who will handle your tax affairs. An advertising campaign during the introduction of self-assessment in 1997 stressed the need to keep full and clear financial records.

This is particularly important now that self-employed people have the opportunity to calculate their own tax bill through self-assessment. Some practitioners, perhaps with the help of an accountant will choose to do this, but those who have complicated finances will prefer to leave the calculations to the Inland Revenue. As an incentive to complete the task themselves, taxpayers are given a longer period of time to complete their paperwork if they agree to calculate their own tax bill. Incidentally the Inland Revenue do plan to check self-assessed tax returns so it is still important to complete the forms accurately. Although the tax offices will still assist with complicated calculations, there are some basic rules you can keep in mind which will make the whole process relatively painless.

Keeping full financial records will assist you when you come to complete your tax return. The Inland Revenue will ask you to disclose self-employed income in one of two ways. Currently if your profit from your practice amounts to less than £15,000 per annum you need only make a short statement of your income and expenditure. Once you exceed this sum you will need to produce more comprehensive accounts broken down into headings such as these:

Income	The total amount of fees from your clients
Cost of sales	What it costs you to run your practice
Employee costs	Do you employ anyone?
Premises	Rent and rates or other costs
Administration	Bookkeepers, secretaries and receptionists
Motor vehicle	Only if you travel regularly to attend a variety of locations but not travel to and from a single place of work
Travel and subsistence	Fares and reasonable costs of overnight stays
Advertising	In directories, leaflets and at conferences
Legal fees	Solicitors and company formation costs
Professionals' fees	Accountants and other professional requirements
Finance charges	Banking and other credit charges

You should ensure that you keep all financial paperwork associated with your business for at least seven years. This includes the information you need to fill in your tax return such as copies of invoices and receipts for all your business transactions, your bank account, loan and credit card statements (which should show all the charges incurred and interest payments made). You will also need personal information such as details of building society mortgage interest paid or savings interest received. Keep to hand your life assurance policies and pension contributions made during the year.

Finance is a worry to many people. Being clear when you can undertake things for yourself and when you need the assistance of a bank manager, accountant, or bookkeeper will free you to concentrate on the core aspects of your practice, namely seeing clients.

Chapter summary

- Time spent planning before you start is a worthwhile investment. Get advice, talk to others, think through the finances before you start to see clients.
- Remember that premises, unless you work from home, will be your single most expensive item.
- Be careful about committing yourself to high supervision costs before your practice is well developed but make sure that the quality and frequency of your supervision is sufficient for your needs.
- Be realistic and don't let your enthusiasm run away with you. Self-employed people are not fee earning the whole time. You will need to take into account holidays, sickness, note taking, accounting and other administration, supervision, therapy and all your travelling time as you set your fees.
- Being cheapest doesn't always get you the most clients, being competitive and realistic about your worth is a better path to success.
- Remember that you only pay income tax on the profit made by your business. That means all your income from client fees, consultancy work (in fact everything except a wage that has been subject to deduction of tax already) less all your genuine business expenses. The more you can justify your expenses as wholly incurred as part of your business, the lower your tax bill will be.
- Keep copies of all your receipts for expenditure and your invoices to your clients.
- Keep a daily cash book. This need not be a complicated document but you should record all your daily business transactions. Record your income received and expenditure incurred, matching it all to your invoices received and fee notes issued
- Note when your business started and decide when you are going to have your year end for accounts. Remember that this may be a different period from the tax year which always runs from 6th April one year to 5th April the next. Your first trading period may be more or less than twelve months. Ask your accountant for advice.
- Government pensions and the National Health Service are funded by National Insurance contributions. If you are self-employed you make a regular contribution each month based on the number of weeks in the month whatever your income. You pay your tax bill half yearly, based on the amount that you have actually earned that year. Once your income exceeds a certain figure, some additional contributions become payable (known as Class 4 contributions) and these are collected along with your income tax.
- It is in your interest to keep your books up to date, or pay someone to do this for you.
- As a general guide start setting aside one-third of your profits in a building society or bank deposit account as soon as you start to make them. Keep this separate from other accounts or transactions and don't be tempted to spend it. This way you will earn some interest (from which the standard rate of tax will already be deducted) which will cover all or most of the tax bill when it comes.

4

Assessments, Contracts, Records and Private Practice

Record keeping

Maintaining clear records of your clients' details and the content of your sessions with them is important for several reasons:

- You need a name, address and telephone contact numbers in case you are unwell or need to change arrangements at short notice.
- Having a written summary of the presenting problem of each client and notes on progress at each session will be helpful for you to refer to as the work develops.
- Once your practice is well established (and as you get older!) you may well find it more difficult to rely on memory to differentiate between clients.
- You will need notes to refer to in supervision.
- Some clients may finish but ask to return at a much later stage, so keeping records will help you pick things up again.
- If there is ever any legal action taken against you by a client it may assist you considerably if you have comprehensive notes in a format that will not incriminate you if they need to be used as evidence in court.

Think about what you need to record. You might consider designing a form so that you can take basic details over the telephone. These days computers and word processors can produce documents quickly and cheaply (but remember you will need to register under the Data Protection Act if you are maintaining information about your clients on a computer).

A name, address and telephone number needs to be obtained at your first contact with the client, and it is not recommended that you see anyone who does not supply this basic information first. True, they could make up an address, but in reality this is unlikely, they are perhaps more likely to ring off without making an appointment when you ask for details. You can at least check the number by calling the client back before the first appointment if you have any concern about the genuineness of the call. It is also useful to know how they heard about your practice, and whether any particular individual or organisation referred them to you.

Next some basic details of the presenting problem would be useful. Taking a lengthy history over the phone is not necessary, but some idea of the issues involved will help and you should write these down. A supply of simply designed forms kept near the telephone can act as a reminder to take down basic information such as name, age, address, phone number and the caller's presenting problem and the following additional suggestions have been made by colleagues:

- Always keep an appointments diary near the telephone.
- Explain what you can offer without appearing to be pushy.
- Leave the choice of whether to make an appointment with the client.
- Don't leave the caller feeling uncared for, even if you cannot help personally.
- Have the number of The Samaritans at hand to pass to distressed callers.
- Consider who answers the phone when you are unavailable and rehearse what they will say.
- Try to ensure that the telephone is answered personally as often as possible.
- Consider how appointments can be made when you are personally unavailable.
- Check that any answering machine message states when you are next available to take calls.

■ If you take calls at home, protect children from distressed callers.

Sometimes practitioners are tested out by the media. For example, members of one psychotherapy group were extremely angry to discover that a member was in fact a journalist who had joined in order to write an article about the group. Needless to say they were well able to express their anger once they discovered how their trust had been broken! New clients do sometimes try to disguise an alternative agenda, but it is particularly difficult to keep this up over a long period of time.

Your next contact will be at the first session, so you will want to record the detail of that interview accurately. It will be useful to refer to at a later date, and provide the basis for discussion with your supervisor.

Some practitioners find it helpful to draw a vertical line down their notebooks. On one side they record what the client says and on the other put their own feelings, their counter-tranference experience and any significant interventions they make.

You will need to agree with your supervisor the exact format of your reporting back, but tape-recorded sessions (with the client's permission of course) or occasional verbatim recording of every word you can remember can be useful. Of course you will not succeed in remembering everything, but you will have a useful exercise to go through in your next supervision bringing insight into your work with your client. It will of course also challenge your listening and remembering skills.

Files

These need not be elaborate, but you will need a filing system which enables you to look back over work with each client. It should provide a good basic record of what has been said and done in the course of each session and be sufficiently portable to take to supervision. Some practitioners use a computerised system but if you do so you will need to be able to print out relevant sections for supervision discussion. Use a password to access the system and for even greater security disguise the identity of your clients. As already mentioned it is important to be aware of the requirement to register under the Data Protection Act if you are keeping computerised information about your clients.

Other practitioners keep a small notebook for each client or clip pages into a small ringbinder. Keep notes, tapes or computer discs securely, preferably locked away. Make sure that your clients cannot be identified from the notes. Refer to them by initials and use a coding or numbering system known only to you. However, make sure this is clearly written down and explained somewhere equally secure but separate from the files. Above all, ask yourself two simple questions whenever you write up your notes.

- How would you feel reading this document out in court in front of your client?
- What would be of most help to your client should sudden illness, incapacity or even death prevent you from working further?

It is possible that a court might one day order you to divulge the contents of a set of client notes. The thought of this keeps the mind focused on your primary intention in making notes in the first place. This should be to record history (who the client is, how they have experienced family life and significant life events to date), process (what was said and how it was responded to in the sessions), moods and feelings (both yours and your clients) interactions and outcomes. You should steer clear of recording hunches, unless you make it quite clear that it is just a hunch. ('I have been seeing this client for six months and my sense is that he relates to me as if I were his mother' not 'I have been seeing this client for six months and he thinks I am his mother.') These differences in recording techniques are important because they say nothing definite about the client which could be then be regarded as libellous. The word 'alleges' is useful here. Newspaper articles always state clearly that a crime has been alleged to have occurred until such time as it is proven in court. This is to protect people who have been accused of a crime and who are subsequently found to be not guilty. Similarly in your client notes never record your client's allegations as fact. You do not know for certain that their neighbour is abusive, only that your client thinks they are. Your notes may accurately cover the client's history, process during sessions, plans for future work and outcomes. Make sure it contains factually correct information. See Jenkins (1997) for further details.

The first interview

Following initial contact, usually by telephone but before deter-
mining a contract with a client it is normal to meet for an initial
interview. This enables both of you to see whether you are able to
work together. This first face-to face contact is an opportunity to
find out why the client has come and to decide together whether
you will be meeting for further sessions. Practice varies, but
usually this is set for something between the traditional fifty-
minute clinical 'hour' and one-and-a-half hours. Make it much
shorter than this and you will not have sufficient information to
complete the task. Make it longer and sessions tend to become
repetitive or tiring for both practitioner and client.

Some people call this an 'intake' session, others an 'assessment'.
'Intake' for me has the connotation of being drawn into something and 'assessment' may imply to some the thought of powerful
professional people deciding what is good for you, possibly
against your will. Neither of these words are particularly useful
when trying to develop a working alliance with your client. I
would suggest referring to it as the 'first interview' or even 'initial
conversation'. This will start you on the process as two equals and
help reduce any anxiety the client may have.

The approach should be one of partnership, exploring how you
and your client together can work out what is going to be best for
them. It needs more than the professional skills of the practitioner
to make a contract. Clients too need to feel free to say whether
they wish to return for future sessions. If a client feels that you are
coercing them into coming back but is unable to say 'no' in the
room, it is quite likely that they will phone to cancel or simply not
keep the next appointment. It is better to allow a client to go
away and think about the commitment that they would be
undertaking.

Someone who does not decide to come back again is not
necessarily resistant. They may simply feel uncomfortable with
any one of a range of issues such as your style, character, location
of premises, gender or personality. It is important to be open to all
these possibilities but at the same time not to take them personally (unless you have discussed them in supervision and discovered that there really are some personal matters for you to
address!).

Where initial interviews are carried out by people who have no direct financial interest in taking on the client themselves, there is a built-in protection which ensures practitioners cannot put their own desire to do business above correct diagnosis. Working privately (especially when not in a partnership) risks the loss of this protection:

Jenny had been in practice for six months, had three clients two of whom ended quite suddenly. Concerned that her supervision costs were now exceeding the fees she received, she was keen to find more clients. When a young woman found her name in the local newspaper classified advertisements she made an appointment. The first interview seemed straightforward enough. The client was well motivated and wanted to work through issues of separation from her mother. At the end of the first session her client mentioned having a special friend in her room at home. There was no time left to explore this so they agreed to meet again the following week. During the next and subsequent sessions the client brought more and more bizarre material, usually towards the end of the session when there was no time to address it properly. It became clear that her client was suffering from a paranoid delusional condition and was in need of proper psychiatric care. With help from her supervisor, Jenny recognised that she had taken on a client who was suffering from a condition beyond the scope of her abilities and who needed more specialised psychiatric help than she could offer. Rather late but before too much damage was done, Jenny recognised her limitations. Her supervisor helped her to see the danger of accepting all newcomers, especially in the early stages of her practice. Sensitively, he also encouraged her to discuss her difficulties in obtaining and keeping clients which had led to her taking on a client without a careful assessment in the first place.

There is a risk that in enthusiasm for business growth, some practitioners will be tempted to take on all comers, whatever the clients' needs, and whatever the capability of the practitioner. Knowing the limitations of your competence and reflecting on them regularly in supervision is especially important in private practice and a good supervisor will help you to address this. The trouble is that it takes courage to discuss these matters frankly when you are starting up and you are keen to get business under way.

There is a range of thinking about charges for initial interviews. Some charge the same as for ongoing sessions. Others offer them free of charge, but this can be seen to undervalue the work. Some practitioners charge an additional fee, recognising that the session may be longer than the normal fifty minute one and there may be more work to do setting up files, considering the case in supervision or researching an appropriate referral. Whatever you charge you need to make your fees clear in advance of meeting your clients.

Practical aspects of first interviews

The first interview is an opportunity to discover why your client has come for help. The meeting should have a therapeutic value for the client and you should use it to find out as much as possible about them. However, it is possible you may not be seeing your client again, so you should be careful not to cause undue disturbance or attachment at this stage.

It is important to recognise that the client may be anxious. They may have had difficulty finding the courage to make an appointment, or had problems in making the journey or finding your consulting room. Many would argue the need to be warm and genuine and to have a positive regard for your client as an individual. Others of a more analytical approach would emphasise the importance of maintaining distance and providing a 'blank screen' for the client's projections. Starting with a silent, analytical style is probably not helpful for most clients; but then neither is an excessively warm and friendly approach. You will need to work out a way that is right for you, integrating a businesslike attitude, professional boundaries and a human response that reflects your philosophy, style and personality.

Above all the client will need to feel heard. You will want to obtain a sense of the client's needs, as well as their personality, history, social environment, lifestyle, strengths and weaknesses. You should be aiming to develop the client's sense of potential within themselves, always allowing the client to move at their own pace and direction.

Paradoxically you will also need to guide your client within a structure that addresses their presenting problem, their life history and the planning of future therapeutic help. Try to facilitate discussion of the presenting problem but beware of repetition. Allow feelings to be discussed and felt, but remember that this may be the only session you have together so the client needs to feel contained by it rather than in pieces at the end. Remember that assessment is not primarily for interpretations, however some trial ones may clarify how the client will respond (Casement, 1985). Note whether the client is able to distinguish feelings from thoughts, and if they are able to face painful thoughts and memories.

As you explore the client's history, address key stage connections with parents, siblings, school and education achievements, work, relationships, marriage, parenthood and ageing. Consider the expectations of their family of origin, their quality of life and whether the client was (or is) central or peripheral to the world of other people. Was their self determination overruled by others?

Towards the end of the session try to find the meeting point of history and of the presenting problem, reflect on whether the story as told to you makes sense. If it does then re-assure the client of this. If it does not then consider what other psychiatric intervention might be appropriate. Where will you go from here, for example will you offer further sessions or a referral elsewhere? Note the mood of the meeting, the personality of the client and the likely prognosis, then any transference or counter-transference feelings generated as you consider the specific aim which you expect the work to have.

Before deciding whether to offer regular appointments you will want to satisfy yourself that there is no gross disturbance such as paranoia, mania, or severe depression in which case a referral to a consultant psychiatrist might be more appropriate. Remember to discuss the practicalities such as the time of appointments, fees, and your policies on charging for missed sessions. By now you will have established the type of service required, be it psychodynamic, person-centred, cognitive or behavioural and noted whether you are trained and equipped to offer what is required yourself.

A good therapeutic alliance will depend upon the capacity of the two of you to relate to one another. Attitudes towards dreams and the unconscious, to transference and counter-transference, ability to symbolise, imagine and laugh, to control impulses and reflect rather than act out will all have a bearing on the potential for working well together if you work psychodynamically. How the client deals with the end of the session will give you insight into their capacity for handling attachment, separation and loss. Finally, remember to write all this up in notes so that you can discuss the case in supervision.

People who have been trained to work in a detached and analytical way may have concerns about being too open or too friendly at the first interview, fearing that disclosing too much of themselves will prevent the development of a useful transference. However, it is also important to see clients as potential customers who will only bring their business to you if they like what you offer, so it makes sense at the very least to be polite, professional, warm and put people at their ease.

Private practitioners who have space in their diaries always have a vested financial interest in accepting and keeping clients. So think about how you will decide in an objective manner whether a particular client would benefit from working with you. You could talk it over with your supervisor, but you may not have immediate access to him/her. Alternatively you might develop a confidential arrangement with a trusted colleague whereby you talk over initial interviews together. This will help to monitor the level of your competence and widen the scope of your potential referral of clients. To be truly objective you could carry out the initial interviews for one another but this is not always practical. Consult Mace (1995) and Palmer and McMahon (1997) for further detailed guidance.

Contracts

It is sensible for practitioners and helpful for their clients to be clear about the type and the quality of service on offer but does this mean that written contracts are a necessity?

Agreeing a contract verbally is a way of conveying trust towards the client. This may be indicated in other ways as well, such as accepting payment by cheque without the need for a bank card, agreeing to bill your established clients with monthly rather than weekly accounts or even lending books to clients. Although none of these may be strictly businesslike, such actions can help clients to feel trusted, something which in turn may help them develop their sense of self worth. Some practitioners would argue that expecting a client to sign a written contract has a detrimental effect from the start, relegating the relationship into pure business. Sills (1997) provides a comprehensive account of all aspects of contracting including its relationship to different theoretical orientations. Also, for a detailed explanation of what is meant by a contract, verbal or written, see Jenkins (1997).

One argument used in favour of contracts is that they can make clear the financial obligations of the client. I have only experienced two clients who have run up small debts and then not settled them. On both occasions I had doubts about their commitment to the work in the first place, but chose to give them the benefit of the doubt. Invoicing clients at the end of each session or by monthly bill ensures that no client is likely to run up excessively large bills. Some practitioners insist on payment in advance but this hardly provides a trusting environment to start with. Non-payment or late payment should be addressed promptly within the sessions and explored at both a practical and an unconscious level. Sometimes it will mask some unexpressed anger towards the therapist, at other times it will simply be that a client's pay cheque has arrived late.

In extreme cases it is possible to use the County Courts for the collection of small debts and these are often agreed through a small claims arbitration service. You may still, however, need to press for payment even once the debt has been proved to exist. You will need some evidence that you agreed a price and provided a service in order for your claim to succeed. If you do not have a written contract with your client then the evidence will be based upon the verbal agreement between you which is unlikely to have been witnessed by anyone else.

The majority of clients, once committed past the first session tend to pay their bills as agreed (few if any practitioners accept payment by credit card as this does nothing to assist the client face the current realities of their life). New clients soon recognise that regular payment at the agreed time (usually monthly or weekly) is part of their necessary commitment to the work.

You might, however, give consideration to written contracts if you are planning to see a significant number of clients each week. In addition to providing a clear description of fees, policy on charging during periods of holiday or sickness, you might wish to include a clear definition of what you mean by confidentiality, times of appointments and how to complain if not satisfied with the quality of service provided. Alternatively some practitioners choose to publish their terms of business in a leaflet form which includes reference to these main points.

In 1996 the British Association for Counselling established a national registration scheme for counsellors (UKRC) and expects its members, whether accredited or not, to sign up to a Code of Ethics and Practice. A United Kingdom Register of Psychotherapists is also in existence. Joining a register and pointing this out to your clients will confirm to them the professional way in which you intend to carry out your business thus helping them to feel confident about using your services.

It is reasonable for a client to ask about your training, experience, qualifications and supervision arrangements, so you should tell them. You may feel able to disclose your own experience of personal therapy, without of course discussing the content. See Dryden and Feltham (1995) for views on what consumers should look for from their own perspective.

Whether a contract is written or verbal there are certain things which should always be included as part of your agreement to work with a client. Having these topics written down makes them clear for both you and your clients however, some clients may not wish to sign a document (particularly if it commits them to a certain number of sessions). Any business relationship should be an open one. It may be tempting to hide behind the transference screen but it is much better to provide clear answers to practical questions as honestly as possible. Of course, counselling and psychotherapy should be an open relationship, one in which client and practitioner alike can be honest with one another and where trust developing over time plays an essential part in the process. For clients who find it difficult to trust others, perhaps because of bad experiences in their upbringing or in relationships with others, you will have an important role in redressing this.

Professionals will want to have a clearly defined Code of Ethics within which to work. The British Association for Counselling has one which is reproduced as a useful example at Appendix 2. Being clear about ethics helps everyone. It defines what practitioners will and will not do in the course of their work, and it confirms to their clients what they may expect in the way of privacy, confidentiality, note taking and keeping, relationships with clients outside the consulting room, supervision and so on.

There is a movement in consumer matters towards providing a clear and unambiguous description of any service before it is purchased. Under the Government's Citizen's Charter initiatives, public services commit themselves to provide an agreed level of service for an agreed price and with an agreed quality. These are measurable qualities (such as the percentage of trains running on time each hour or the number of minutes before an accident and emergency doctor sees a patient). In private practice clients' expectations about therapy will vary. Some will arrive distressed and ready to talk straightaway with little or even no interest in your qualifications or experience. Others will want to know what you offer in more detail. Some will want to hear from you that your type of therapy will definitely work for them. The reality is that people do benefit from therapy of differing types; it is important neither to offer nor imply any kind of guarantee. Therapy has to work as a partnership between practitioner and client. When for example you purchase a television, you expect it to be in working order and able to receive all available channels, but you do not have any guarantee about the quality of programmes broadcast. Similarly, counselling or psychotherapy clients may expect you to keep appointments, to be on time for sessions, to listen and respond appropriately, and generally support their quest for personal growth and self-awareness. But you can never predict the final outcome for any one individual so it is essential not to make promises about this. Incidentally, if you and your clients accept that your work is primarily about developing a clinical relationship and this is as much an art as it is a science then there will be less need for categorical proof of likely outcomes.

Even if you decide to offer a verbal contract only, it is helpful to have your terms of business printed. A leaflet setting out terms of business can either be posted to clients prior to meeting or handed to them at the first interview. The advantage in posting it is twofold. First, it can also include details of where the practice is situated, perhaps a map, directions and local transport arrangements. Second, experience tends to show that clients who receive a letter confirming the appointment tend to be more likely to keep it than those who make an appointment on the telephone only. It only takes a moment to put a confirmation in the post and this gives the client an initial introduction to you and to the service you provide. It looks businesslike and shows that you are taking care of the arrangements in a professional manner. If you do choose to produce a formal contract you should discuss the detail of it with a solicitor.

Chapter summary

- Clients may be anxious on arrival; how will you greet them?
- Will you offer a verbal or a written contract?
- Contracts or literature need to define the terms of your business.
- What records will you be keeping on your clients?
- What will you want to achieve from the initial interview with each client?
- Consider including a statement of where you work; a brief description of the kind of therapy you offer; the Code of Ethics to which you subscribe and how to complain.
- Explain the length and times of your appointments; your fees and terms of business especially your policy on charging for cancelled sessions and holidays.

5

Premises and Private Practice

Home or away?

When considering premises the first thing to resolve is whether you want to work at home or in a separate consulting room. Some practitioners are fortunate to have premises which they can combine both as a home and a private practice. A large house that has been used as a vicarage or a doctor's surgery and has a separate study or consulting room already might be an ideal investment if you have a family but want to be close to your work. These are relatively rare to find and usually much more expensive than an average home. Alternatively, some practitioners have converted property for example by constructing an extension with a separate entrance, or sacrificing their garage for an additional room.

Roof space can sometimes be converted but this is not always easily accessible and can be a particular problem for claustrophobic or obese clients. Not everyone will be able to climb two or three flights of stairs, and using an attic or loft conversion will inevitably mean that clients will pass through every level of your home on the way in and again on the way out.

If you live alone, it may be somewhat easier for you to use your living room as a consulting room too, but this will depend on whether you are prepared to share your home space with your clients. For most people of modest means the only space available at home will be their living room. This need not be a problem, provided that arrangements are handled sensitively. You will of course want the room to be clean, tidy and welcoming, but not giving away too many traces of your private life.

If you do decide to work from home, you will need to ask yourself two equally important questions:

- How much disruption will your work have on your family?
- How much disruption will your family have on your work?

The family's needs

The ages and attitudes of the rest of your household need to be taken into account. Does everyone living in your home, including your partner, spouse, young children or older relatives, really understand the work that you are doing? Are they able to give their full consent to the effect that it may have on their lives? You will need to have an honest discussion with your family about this before you start. Think in advance about the reasonable sounds that will emanate from a family. Can people have a shower in the bathroom if it is next to your consulting room? Can babies cry (they will anyway!)? Can children watch TV? How will you feel if your teenage son picks an argument with his sister or your cat is sick on the hall carpet just as your client is arriving?

Small children and even older ones do not always understand why their parent should spend long periods of time with clients rather than with them. Many spouses or partners also find it stressful having strangers entering the family home and this can lead to conflict. Sometimes this can only be resolved by seeing clients away from the home which will add to the costs of the practice. It is better to be realistic about this before you start to see clients (Maeder, 1990).

Not everyone will react in the same way to the proposal to see clients at home:

Jamie was a therapist working from home and getting under his wife's feet. She wanted him to go out and get a 'proper' job, resented the times he was cloistered with female clients for fifty minutes at a time. However, careful timetabling meant that he was always available to pick the children up from school. Janice, on the other hand was a full time mother who fitted in a few hours counselling on a Tuesday evening at home. She would see her clients after handing the children over to her husband. He and the

*children enjoyed the arrangement as it gave them a regular
time alone with each other.*

Some people appreciate the saving of time which would otherwise be spent commuting to work, others need the structure of
travel and a working day in a different environment. Working
successfully from home will depend on mutual understanding,
clear communication and joint acceptance of the limitations as
well as the benefits encountered by all involved (see Feltham,
1995b).

The clients' needs

Consider also the effect which a home environment would have
on your clients. Are there lavatory facilities they can use? Would
you allow a client to phone for a lift, especially if you were a long
way from public transport? What would you do if their car broke
down? Where would they wait if they arrived early or were
waiting for a taxi, especially if you had another client due and it
was raining outside?

Clients will have no choice about the location in which you
choose to work. How then will each of your clients react to noise,
music and the traits of family life going on around them? Some will
scarcely notice, while others will be constantly distracted. You
will need to weigh up these points when making a decision about
where to work. A quiet consulting room away from home may
appear more professional to some but rather clinical to others.
Alternatively, working from home will be viewed as pleasantly
informal by some while others may regard it as amateur.

Location is one of the most important decisions you will have to
face before you start your practice. Planning now for the future
expansion of your practice will mean that you are less likely to
have to move your location at a later date. For many clients a
change of room can be difficult so this is best avoided or at least
planned well in advance. However, many practitioners start
from home, build a viable practice and then take on business
premises.

Home life and transference

If you work analytically, from your own home, and focus much of
your work within the transference you will need to consider how

much knowledge of you and your family you are prepared to share. Do you feel it is important to keep the client completely unaware of your partner or family life, or is it rather unrealistic to do so? Will you see them in a room at home that at other times is used for family life? One therapist regularly removed his wedding ring before sessions until one day his wife discovered and protested loudly! Will there be family photographs or toys lying around? Will you use clients' comments about these things as part of the work or will you hastily tidy up before they arrive? It is always possible to work with the material the client brings, even if it is a reaction to our own environment. Being a 'blank screen' may help a client to get in touch with their inner feelings and fantasies but carried to excess in a home setting this is neither helpful to the client nor realistic.

Planning and consent issues

Wherever you work, it is important to consider any rules or regulations which may affect your ability to practise. These fall into four primary areas:

- Restrictions placed upon you by your landlord (lease).
- Restrictions placed upon you by the person who sold you the property (covenants).
- Restrictions placed by your local authority (planning consent).
- The effect of your work upon your neighbours.

Landlords

If you work in rented premises, you should check the terms of your agreement with your landlord. You may need to explain to your landlord precisely what seeing clients at home would involve because there may be a clause in your rent agreement preventing you from working at home at all. A private practice is normally a quiet activity which has little more effect on your neighbours or landlord than any other regular visits to your home. But sometimes a landlord will need reassurance.

Denise worked with a drug helpline service which had obtained funding for its work, but had difficulty in obtaining suitable premises as there was concern expressed by potential landlords about possible anti-social activity. Once it was made clear that most of the work would be carried out by telephone, and only accompanied recovering addicts would be admitted to the premises, a rental agreement was reached.

Covenants

If you purchased your premises, somewhere in the original deeds there may be specific agreements or covenants compelling you to, or preventing you from doing certain things.

Sandra, the owner of a nursing home, was moving into larger local premises so she placed a covenant in the deeds of the old property to prevent the purchaser from setting up a competing nursing home. The value of the property was reduced because it could only be used for different purposes.

In my own home I am expressly forbidden to operate a funfair roundabout in my garden, which I have no intention of doing, but this was probably of serious concern to the owner of the original site and the first neighbours who moved into the houses some eighty years ago. Consequently, covenants do become out of date and irrelevant to the current uses of the land. It is unlikely that there is a covenant covering the use of your home for counselling or psychotherapy practice, but there might be restrictions on general business activities. Unless your home is very recently built, it is also unlikely that anyone is going to challenge you should you breach a covenant, but it is worth checking your deeds to be certain. In cases of doubt ask a solicitor. It may be possible to purchase very cheaply an indemnity insurance against any future challenge.

Local authority

You pay council tax on the basis that your premises are for residential use. If you significantly change their use to business premises you will be liable to business rates on that part of the property which you use to see clients. On the other hand, seeing a couple of clients at home for money one evening a week can hardly be deemed to be significant business use, and may well be regarded by a sympathetic authority as no more than a profitable hobby.

Government policy is on your side because in recent years local authorities have been encouraged to adopt a relaxed approach to people starting up new businesses. There is a world of difference between repairing motorbikes in your garage at all hours of the day and night and spending a few hours each week in conversation with your clients. You should talk to your local planning officer about this who will explain local planning arrangements and relevant restrictions.

The greatest public nuisance caused by the practice of counselling or psychotherapy in people's homes is the frequent arrivals and departures. These may cause parking, access and noise problems and you should be ready to demonstrate that you have thought of these issues in advance, perhaps by not seeing clients after 9 pm or making parking space available for clients' cars. Being open with your neighbours is sensible and avoids the misunderstanding experienced at one location where neighbours thought that the regular arrivals and departures indicated the practitioner was running a brothel!

Hiring a room

Working from home will not always be practical and to keep costs to a minimum, you could hire a room by the hour, perhaps negotiating over some local office space that has been empty for a while, or seeing if there is a room available at certain times of the day at a GP or dental practice, church or community hall.

There may be a counselling centre or alternative health clinic nearby which will allow you to use rooms on an hourly basis and if you establish a good relationship this may lead to referrals as well.

It is also possible to hire premises on a licensed basis. This is a useful arrangement for new businesses because one payment normally includes facilities such as a secretary, telephone, fax, security and cleaning costs as well as the rental and business rates. A short notice period, perhaps even just one month may be agreed.

Choosing premises

Will sound carry significantly through the walls? When visiting to assess suitability you should always take someone along with you. Your friend can help you check on the quality of soundproofing by both talking and listening in the room as you listen and talk in adjacent rooms. Alternatively, a portable radio placed in the next room will give you some idea of how sound travels. Visit at a variety of times, both during the day and the evening. While a factory or office next door may be quieter in the evenings, a pub or night-club will certainly be noisier. Noise from street level (passing traffic and pedestrians) will also vary considerably with the time of day.

It is probably better to use a room facing away from road and pedestrian areas (even if it means one without a view). Carpeted corridors help to cut down on sound but they should not be in constant use. Corner rooms may cost more to heat but may be quieter if they have fewer adjoining walls. Check what actually happens in the next room or office and the ones above or below.

You will need lavatory facilities and somewhere to make drinks and wash up. Enquire about cleaning arrangements, both for your own room and for any communal areas and the cost of these facilities if they are shared.

While needing a confidential and reasonably soundproofed setting, this should not be so secure as to leave you entirely out of earshot of other people. So check whether the landlord provides security patrols at night or weekends or whether there are reception facilities available. In extreme circumstances you may need to be able to call out for help so it may give you added confidence to know that there is someone else nearby.

Check that you are free to decorate and furnish the room to your own taste and that there is room for a couch or chairs, perhaps a desk and a small table for tissues, a clock and so on. Will you be able to get furniture upstairs or in a lift if necessary? Premises do not need to be large, just adequate for seating two or three people at a time in comfort, although you will need more space if you work with families or groups. Art therapists in particular may need extra room for storage and use of paint, paper and other materials.

You are likely to have a higher demand for your services if your practice is in or near a large town or city. Remember though that there will be more competition for clients and that accommodation will in turn be more expensive. A recent British Association for Counselling's *Directory of Counselling and Psychotherapy Resources* lists 649 practitioners in London but only six in the whole of Cornwall! Renting a room will give you the opportunity to place your practice where your clients are without having to move home. There are many examples of psychotherapists and counsellors having a small practice at home and another in a major city. At least one commutes weekly between Leicester and London and finds it worth his while to pay out additional costs of travel and room hire in the capital in order to charge the higher fees that London clients are prepared to pay.

However, not all clients will have their own transport, so are your premises on a bus route or near a railway station? Is there parking available on site or nearby? It is thoughtful to have some secure space available where a client can park a bicycle. Is it easy to find and in a safe public area but with a discreet way of obtaining access? Is it well lit at night? Bear in mind that clients may well shy away from visiting seedy or impoverished areas, especially on dark evenings.

Signage is important, both of the premises and of your presence within them. On any exterior sign it is better to have a clear reference to the full address or name of the building which you give to new clients. A large sign stating 'So-and-So's Psychotherapy Service' may embarrass clients but a discreet name board in an entrance hall or on a brass plate beside the bell is helpful. Is there a door buzzer or entryphone system to which you can respond from your room?

Ideally clients should not be expected to explain their presence to receptionists, security guards or other people who are unconnected with your practice before they can be let in to see you, but if this is unavoidable you should ensure that staff understand the importance of confidentiality and respect for clients.

It may seem obvious to point out that most clients will have experienced some distress in their lives. You should therefore try to make the location and ambience of your consulting room as user-friendly as possible. Factors such as location and lighting are important, but so is the ability of a client suffering from claustrophobia to be able to get up and leave. Some may have strong fears of being trapped and this can be exacerbated by the shape of the room or placing of furniture. Consider whether the door is easily accessible to the client. Does it need to be locked during a session to preserve confidentiality and to prevent interruption or would the client find this intimidating?

How would you cope with a fire alarm during a session with your client? Fire instructions should be clearly displayed and you should of course know where to find the nearest fire exits and extinguishers. Whether it is a real emergency or a false alarm, you will need to consider the safety of your client and yourself. You may be thrown together in a street or other public area for a considerable time while the emergency is resolved which may make it impossible to retain normal boundaries between you. Your client may not thank you for keeping silent or maintaining the therapist role in a real emergency so having a pre-planned strategy of what to say and do on such an occasion will prove helpful.

Ambience

All national chains of shops pay great attention to providing a pleasant and welcoming shopping environment, recognising that in so doing customers will be encouraged to make purchases. Similarly, if we think of our private consulting room as our shop, then we too should be creating a pleasant, clean, quiet and secure place to talk.

I once worked with a charity that provided evening counselling in a room that was occupied by a mother and baby welfare group during the daytime. I was literally surrounded by old prams, children's clothes and nappy packs, but it was remarkable how few clients commented on the surroundings. Clients seemed to be so pleased to have somewhere that they could talk about their problems that they scarcely noticed the contents of the room at all. However, they were not paying private fees.

You should use premises in which your clients feel comfortable and contained and where you feel safe and creative. Clients will be more likely to use sessions productively if they are not distracted by noise or jazzy colours. They need to gain confidence in you as well as feel comfortable sitting in your armchair or lying on your couch. If you sit face to face, angle the chairs slightly so that you are not directly confrontational. This gives clients the chance to look away every so often without having to evade your eye contact. If you use a couch, make sure that you have a freshly painted ceiling, for your clients will be spending hours focusing on the cracks and cobwebs above!

Clients need to feel at home, and although you are unlikely to know much about their living environment, you can give some thought to providing one which is reasonably welcoming. An open fire on a cold day, or fresh flowers in the summer all help to make the room cheerful without being too distracting.

Jung liked to use the mandala as a symbol of wholeness and an aid to meditation and deep reflection. If you visit the museum in Freud's house in London you will see how he preferred the complicated Turkish patterns on carpets and rugs that were fashionable in the 1930s. Unless you are an art therapist or a humanistic practitioner engaging in expressive work with clients you should avoid excessively bright colours especially blues, reds and yellows. When re-decorating consider colours that are neither garish nor dull, but provide warmth and tranquillity such as the autumnal shades of orange and brown or pastoral shades of green. This will help to create a tranquil and peaceful atmosphere.

Think too about the message you will give to different clients when they arrive. John was looking for a training analysis:

I tried two therapists. The first was strictly analytic in style. She did not come to the front door but expected me to walk in when a buzzer sounded. The room was immaculately clean and beautifully furnished with antiques and china ornaments. There was no greeting and no response when I said why I had come. I'd just become a father and I had hoped that she would have some idea of what it was to be a young parent developing a career, but I doubt whether she had ever had children and certainly thought I could never bring my inner 'mess' here. My second attempt was better. There were kids bikes in the hallway and the furniture seemed a little worn. Occasionally there might be a jigsaw puzzle left out on the table. Unlike my experience with the first therapist I felt I could be myself there.

A quiet or reserved single person might well have chosen the first therapist, and found the second one to be a painful reminder of their loneliness. There is no right and wrong way for much will depend on individual tastes and personality. But the purpose of these examples is not to tell you how to decorate your room, but to set you thinking about the kind of message your decor gives to others (see Rowan, 1988).

Access for people with a disability

In considering premises you should also think about your policy towards people with a disability. The Disability Discrimination Act which is being implemented in stages proposes that people must not be offered a worse service because they have a disability. This Act of Parliament may have little effect on self-employed businesses, as it is aimed at businesses with twenty or more employees, however, it does raise the question of good practice. Consider disability under three headings, namely physical, sensory and learning disabilities.

Physical access

Modern premises should already be designed for good wheelchair access. If you are considering new premises, before committing yourself consider whether there is level, wheelchair access through doors that are wide enough and a lift if you are not on the ground floor. If you already have premises which are not easily accessible, you could consider making special arrangements at another location. Your social services department or local branch of a disability organisation may be able to offer advice on what is available locally, or even provide a suitable location so that you do not have to refuse to see a client simply because access to your premises is difficult.

Recent changes in legislation also mean that people with a disability may be able to seek direct funding for their personal care. This gives more choice in the way they spend their money, rather than simply being passive receivers of services. For some this may mean choosing to use counselling, advice and advocacy services.

Sensory impairment

This primarily refers to hearing and visual impairment and includes people who are completely deaf or blind. These disabilities bring challenges to traditional methods of communication in counselling and psychotherapy. For example, visual impairment can be overcome for some clients by producing large type literature about your services or information on tape or in Braille.

Large black print on yellow paper stands out well and is the easiest format for a partially sighted person to read. Give some thought to how you can make your premises safe for someone with a sensory impairment. For example, many hazards that are obvious to a sighted person such as a rug edge or lamp flex may be dangerous or even lethal for someone who is blind. Apart from safety in physical access to premises, blindness has no effect on a client's ability to use therapy. In fact people with a visual impairment often have better access to their inner world of imagination and self-reflection than sighted people.

Deaf or hard of hearing clients may have learned to lip-read and simply need you to speak slowly and distinctly. Raising your voice won't help as much as an induction loop. This is a device which will help them use a hearing aid on your premises and a minicom (providing text communication over the phone) could be of value. If this seems too expensive consider purchasing a moveable system which you could share with other practitioners locally and then advertise its availability.

Sometimes counsellors are asked to see a client with a sign language interpreter present and are concerned about issues of confidentiality. However, this should not be of concern since there is a strict code of conduct among British Sign Language interpreters which ensures that the interpreter keeps confidential all information heard during interpretation. Your local social services department should have details of how to contact signers and you could discuss with them how to offer special counselling facilities to people with disabilities.

Learning disabilities

Having a learning disability (once more frequently referred to as mental handicap) relates to clients who have an intellectual impairment. In practice many people with a learning disability are potential clients but may be prevented from using private counselling or psychotherapy services because they have neither the ability to make the arrangements nor the financial resources to pay for them. Keeping appointments may also be difficult without the support of a friend, family or a social worker. However, some very effective work has been done with people who either have a learning disability or speech problem by using interpreted activity such as art therapy or sand play. Providing there is a clear arrangement in place for the funding of treatment (perhaps with the local health or social services department) there is no reason why someone with such a disability should not attend for regular sessions, if necessary with a sensitive advocate or carer who understands when to stay in and when to remain outside the room. Successful practitioners in this area of work have had suitable specialist training and experience. In general terms having a mild learning disability should not in itself be a bar to becoming a client.

Mencap locally or nationally can give advice about working with people with learning difficulties and there is also a growing awareness among people with mild learning disabilities of the importance of being able to speak out for themselves through organisations such as People First. Although their prime aim is advocacy rather than counselling it is very much in tune with the counselling ethos of assisting people to make decisions for themselves rather than accept whatever is thrust upon them by society.

Practitioners who have a disability

It may be that you have a disability yourself. If so, you will want to think carefully about whether you make this clear to your potential clients.

> *Pat was a counsellor with multiple sclerosis. She advertised in directories as being a wheelchair user, thinking that it would attract clients who were similarly disabled, especially as she had premises which were wheelchair accessible. Very few clients contacted her and certainly not enough to sustain a private practice. Janice was a psychotherapist and also a wheelchair user but simply had her directory entry listed as wheelchair accessible with no mention of her own disability. Knowing that there is prejudice and ignorance about disability in society, Janice decided to be open, acknowledging the genuine surprise of her clients when she opened the door in a wheelchair and being prepared to discuss any concerns that a client might have about her ability to provide a professional service. More people came to see Janice than Pat.*

Telephone

The telephone is an essential aspect of your business and to avoid unnecessary expenses you will need to plan carefully how to get the greatest benefit from it. You will be unable to receive calls when you are seeing clients, and nor will you want to have calls at home in the middle of the night, so it is important to consider how you will offer an efficient service when you are not personally available.

If you are working from home, you would be well advised to have a separate line for your clients. You will need to plan this well in advance as many directories take at least a year to change a listing, and people will continue to use old directories well after that. You may not need to use the additional line for many calls out, so it need not necessarily be expensive. As the British Telecom monopoly has been broken, and many suburban subscribers are offered an alternative cable telephone provider, the costs tend to fall anyway. A specific business line will cost a little more, but it will bring with it a free Yellow Pages listing. Most classified directories such as Yellow Pages and Thompson Directories have recently begun including sections for counsellors and psychotherapists. Experience suggests, however, that they tend to produce more enquiries from people wanting to sell services than clients seeking them. Also many people tend to misread 'psychotherapy' as 'physiotherapy', leading to rather confusing conversations about the relative merits of psychotherapy treatment upon various parts of the human anatomy!

By having a separate line for your clients you will always know whether the incoming call is business or personal. If you have young children you can safely allow them to answer the personal line without fear that they may pick up the business phone and be left dealing with a distressed client. If you have teenagers in the house who are likely to spend considerable periods of time on the telephone (especially in the early evenings when some clients may call) a separate line will ensure your business calls are not blocked. Alternatively for less than the cost of a new line it is possible to have a 'call waiting' tone added to your line so that when your line is engaged and someone else is trying to get through you will hear a tone.

To keep your personal life completely uninterrupted, simply fit an answering machine to your business line. The line does not have to be installed at your consulting room; you might find it more convenient to take calls at home, or have a family member answer the calls for you, especially while you are seeing clients. Late messages can be sent to a mobile phone or to a message pager (but remember to switch them off during sessions).

It is always better to offer a personal reply on the telephone whenever you can. Even ordinary domestic telephone systems offer call re-direct services so that you can take calls at home in the evening or have them redirected to your office during the day from the same number. If the reality is that you can only take calls after say six o'clock, then it is better to say so in your advertising and on your answering machine.

Chapter summary

- Decide whether to work from home or elsewhere.
- Choose the area and location of premises carefully.
- Remember the importance of soundproofing.
- Consider whether clients will conflict with home life.
- Be aware of the issues of transference when working from home.
- Understand the legal implications of where you work.
- Look objectively at the ambience of the room in which you work.
- Think about disability issues including safe and easy access to premises.
- Make the best use of the telephone.

6

Safety, Boundaries, Insurance and Private Practice

Keeping safe

In conversation with other practitioners about personal safety most of them have had a tale to tell about clients who have caused anxiety at some stage in their work. These are by no means everyday experiences, however it is important to be prepared for handling clients who are out of the ordinary in their behaviour. Some will clearly be in need of specialist psychiatric services and the importance of having access to a consultant psychiatrist for seriously disturbed clients has already been stressed in Chapter 1. (See also Daines et al., 1997.) Others may simply be excessively angry, distressed or strange in their behaviour. Some may wish to talk about sex for self-arousal rather than to gain insight, while others have been known to arrive high on drugs or alcohol. Most clients will be far too concerned about their own problems to pose any threat to you, so it is important to keep a sense of proportion but you should nevertheless think through issues of personal safety before you start to practise, especially if you work alone or in a relatively isolated place.

Risk assessment

Before you practise it is wise to have a fully thought out policy for risk assessment. As a starting point you will need to be clear about what you can and cannot tolerate in a client's behaviour. Just because there is always some risk involved in providing a therapeutic relationship, this does not mean that you should put yourself in unnecessary danger or accept intolerable behaviour from clients. I mention this because in trying to understand clients it is possible to lose objectivity and fail to recognise when we are simply being unacceptably abused by them.

Boundaries

You may decide to work like most others to the fifty minute 'clinical hour'. Clients will often try to push the boundaries, thinking of very important issues just as the session is about to finish, and you will need to keep your wits (and a clock) about you if you are to be firm with endings. Words like, 'We will need to continue this discussion next time' are actually quite containing, although you should not expect the client to thank you for them at the time. But you should not be so rigid and controlling as to be out of touch with the client's distress. Providing it does not affect other clients who may be waiting, it may well be acceptable on a very few occasions to allow a deeply distressed client to sit quietly and regain their composure before they leave, even if this means going a few minutes over their allotted time.

This is quite different from coping with a client who sits tight at the end of a session and refuses to move out of the room. You may have tried being firm and reminding the client that they can continue next time all to no avail. You may recognise that they are in a distressed state or that they are acting out some temper tantrum from their childhood but your interpretations are not hitting home. Do you simply remain silent and refuse to respond to them? Do you walk out, leaving them behind in the room? Do you try to physically remove them from the room with the risk of a charge of assault? Do you allow yourself to become angry (or does this seem unprofessional)? Do you summon help from someone else, or even call the police and in the process break confidence? If you have a client waiting do you allow the first one to delay your work, or do you signal the next client to enter as a clear statement that you have finished with the first? It may be that some cooling off time is needed and that any interpretations or further discussion will have to wait for a later session. There is no simple answer to what to do in these circumstances and much will depend on your judgement of the situation, but you will be better prepared if you think about these things in advance.

Keeping your boundaries clear will help to contain clients and keep them focused on the work. So keep your life separate from your clients as far as you are able. This means not accepting referrals from within your own group of colleagues, friends, neighbours and others you know well. Before you take on any client, always ask yourself whether you are likely to have even occasional contact with the client in other areas of your life. This can be a problem in small towns and rural areas, but normally you would do better to refer such people on to someone else.

Sex and clients

The British Association for Counselling has concluded that it is unethical to have a sexual relationship with a client and that even after ending counselling, counsellors remain accountable for relationships with former clients and must 'exercise caution over entering into friendships, business relationships, sexual relationships, training and other relationships' (BAC *Code of Ethics and Practice for Counselling* – see Appendix 2). Some but not all professional bodies place an outright ban on sex with current or past clients. Common sense dictates that such a relationship after a period of therapy can never be one of equal partnership and that there will always be the risk that unresolved issues from the therapy are being acted out in the relationship. Sometimes, however, there is a fine line between positive transference and falling in love. Anyone who does form a close personal relationship with one of their clients needs in any case to withdraw from providing a professional service to that client. It is their own responsibility to discuss ending the work sensitively in the course of their supervision, if necessary referring the client on to someone else.

Angry clients

How would you deal with an angry client, one who was really shouting at the top of their voice? What effect might this have on the staff in the office next door, the family in the next room or your neighbours? How would this affect the way you dealt with the client? Would you avoid stirring up issues that made your client angry, or would you accept that they needed help in dealing with the underlying cause of their anger? How do you respond to anger in others generally? Is it something you can tolerate or does it have such a negative effect on you that you would be unable to continue working with such clients? Clients will get angry at times, perhaps directing their anger at others if not at you. It may require careful interpretation, which when accurate can release tension and help the client to deal with their feelings. But it can also be highly embarrassing and distressing to others nearby.

Being on the receiving end of anger can be frightening, especially for a practitioner working alone. You will therefore need to assess the risk perceived from each client. Someone who is able to express strong feelings through words may be less likely to be physically violent than the frustrated person who cannot find the words to express themselves. So it may be possible to tolerate extreme anger in a client as long as that anger is not acted out as violent behaviour against yourself or others.

Some practitioners working in the humanistic tradition such as Gestalt or Primal Therapy may actively encourage their clients to express anger and other strong feelings. In this case extra sound-proofing placed within an appropriate location is called for so that clients may freely express themselves.

Violent clients

Some clients may become violent and it is not always possible to predict which ones, but you can be prepared by thinking out in advance how the furniture and other objects in the room are placed. Is there anything such as a heavy lamp or candlestick which might be used as a weapon against you? Do you have anything suitable to hand to defend yourself if necessary? Are you nearest to the door if you should need to escape quickly? While you would not wish to have a telephone ringing obtrusively in the room during your session, you should consider the importance of having access to a telephone during sessions. In an emergency you may need to call 999 but you should also keep the numbers handy for contacting the local police, psychiatric services, the community mental health team or social services. The number for The Samaritans too can be useful for passing on to clients who may telephone in a suicidal state or have difficulty in coping with the gaps between sessions.

Protecting yourself and clients

Ideally, you should always have someone present in the building where you see clients. This might be a partner or family member if you are working from home and receptionist in an office accommodation. There should always be someone close enough to be within earshot (or by an internal telephone) but far away enough not to be able to eavesdrop on conversation at a normal level of sound. Two rooms away might be an ideal position, depending of course on factors such as the thickness of walls. That way they would be able to come to your aid if you needed to raise your voice or sound an alarm.

Clients may become ill or injured, so keep a first aid box handy in the room where you see them. Obviously you should call an ambulance for anything serious but attending a course run by The Red Cross or St John's Ambulance Service will give you life saving knowledge of how to deal with sudden problems such as choking, heart attack, diabetic coma or epileptic fit. Also the Suzy Lamplugh Trust works hard to highlight the issues of personal safety and produces useful literature which is relevant for anyone meeting strangers as part of their work.

Raising the alarm

Personal attack alarms are cheap to purchase and loud when let off, but it is equally important that anyone who might be asked to come to your aid recognises the signal emitted and clearly understands the appropriate response to make. Some rehearsal is advisable.

If you consider that setting off a noisy alarm in the room would agitate a client further you could pre-arrange a coded distress call for assistance. Telephones with the ability to dial a pre-programmed number at the touch of one or two buttons are available. All mobile phones have this facility and although more expensive are smaller and therefore easier to keep out of sight, for example in a handbag, inside pocket or down the side of a chair. Modern phones pick up surrounding conversation very well, or you could agree on a distress code word, one that you might well use frequently in the course of any session. Make certain that the person you arrange to receive the call is always actually available during your sessions and knows exactly what to do if they receive a distress call from you.

Tape recording for safety

I have mentioned that some practitioners (with their client's consent) tape record sessions. As well as being useful for supervision and future reflection on the work, it can also provide a measure of protection as clients may be less likely to behave aggressively if they know that their conversation will be recorded. Such use should be carefully considered however and not resorted to lightly.

Know your clients

You should always get as a minimum the name, address and telephone number of your client over the telephone. It may be helpful to know whether they are married or in a stable relationship and you may wish to ask their age if you are not certain whether they are over eighteen. As with all aspects of counselling and psychotherapy you should only work within the limits of your own competence so only work with children if you are trained to do so.

You cannot eliminate the possibility of them giving you a false name and address but I would not advise anyone to see a client who refuses to give these basic details about themselves. Some clients may need reassurance about telephone calls being returned to their home (or work) number, so you may need to confirm that you will not under any circumstances disclose your professional relationship with them to any third party including their partner or spouse.

Ideally you should take clients only from known sources of referral such as colleagues, professional bodies, training institutions, health service practitioners such as consultants and GPs, or well established organisations. Bodies such as the NHS services and reputable counselling agencies will already have details of their clients on file.

You should be additionally wary of any clients who come to you from any form of public advertising. Advertising in general directories, in cards in shop windows and classified advertisements will open up your practice to all comers. This may be tempting, especially when starting up but the more widely you advertise your services, the more aware you need to be about the clients you see. Experience shows that few people seriously seeking professional help approach their counsellors or psychotherapists in this way. Such clients may not be fully motivated to attend or to work in partnership with the practitioner when they do. They may have no real understanding of what to expect, imagining that you will provide advice or a panacea for all their problems.

Any general advertising like this will also expose you to the risk of working with mental health service patients who have discharged themselves from the psychiatric services against professional advice. Private practitioners are particularly vulnerable to approaches from such patients, especially where their level of paranoia causes them to believe that their psychiatrists or other professionals are working against their interests.

False accusation

Personal safety is an issue for both women and men, for while women may be the more likely targets of physical or sexual attacks by their clients, men may carry the risk of being falsely accused of inappropriate sexual or physical behaviour towards their female clients. Trainee ministers of religion, predominantly males as recently as the 1960s, were taught to leave their vestry or study door open when they were alone with a woman. Counsellors and psychotherapists simply could not operate on that basis as it would compromise the confidential nature of their relationship with clients. However, it takes just one client charged with a vivid imagination to destroy a career by accusation of professional misconduct, so this is another reason to keep carefully compiled casenotes.

Suicidal clients

Suicidal clients and those at risk of doing other harm to themselves need special attention. It is not just the client's but the welfare of the practitioner that is at risk, for it can be extremely distressing if a client commits suicide. Some precautions can help to reduce the risk, if not prevent this from happening altogether.

You should have a plan for dealing both with unknown people who contact you feeling suicidal and for existing clients who become suicidal in the course of the work.

If you receive a call from someone who appears to be at immediate risk of suicide or self-harm, it is better to recognise the client's distress immediately and clarify what you can and cannot offer. An appointment for an interview in a week or two is unlikely to be of help, you cannot offer a twenty-four hour helpline to callers; this is better left to organisations such as The Samaritans. Keep their number beside the phone; they are always willing to listen, day or night. You should also advise a caller to contact their doctor, either for medication or referral to a consultant psychiatrist. You may need prompt access to specialist help which will normally come from your psychiatric consultant or local psychiatric hospital.

Sometimes an existing client may become so distressed during the course of therapy that you may fear they might harm themselves. Whether a client is at genuine risk of self-harm or using the threat of such to gain attention makes no difference. Prompt and skilled intervention is called for. An additional emergency session might be appropriate for a long-term client working through difficult feelings but you may not be able to offer this. You need to encourage your client to seek psychiatric help, through their GP or your own psychiatric consultant if they do not already have one. Many people suffering from mental illness do not recognise their need for help and may at first refuse to do this. You should not be afraid of making it a condition of any continuing treatment that you work with their doctor or psychiatrist to ensure the best quality of treatment. Explain that you need permission to contact their medical adviser. Some practitioners insist on having the name of a client's GP (or especially a psychiatric consultant if there is one) as a condition of working with any client, and routinely obtain this at their first interview. Say that it is in their interest to ensure that the care you are each providing is appropriate, fits together in a helpful package, and that you are not duplicating one another's efforts. In this way your objectives will be recognised by all parties involved. Of course some clients may be too ill to understand this or too wary to give you permission, but they are unlikely to benefit from counselling or psychotherapy anyway. Others will appreciate the care that you are taking. Either way it is still important to recognise the value of all the different professionals, including yourself, and act together.

Not all clients will deny the seriousness of their condition. Some may be relieved that you have recognised their symptoms and that you are able to confirm their urgent need of help. Remember it is never unethical to break confidence where the life of the client or anyone else is at stake. See Jenkins (1997) for further clarification.

Insurance

National Insurance contributions, towards sickness and state pensions are compulsory for most people, but provide only the most basic cover. You should consider purchasing a personal pension plan, life cover and health insurance. There are plenty of schemes to choose from and you should seek the advice of a broker.

You may be able to cover small breaks off work yourself, perhaps from savings but you should also consider what the impact of a long-term illness or a disability would have on your practice. For counsellors or psychotherapists a sudden or even progressive loss of hearing could bring their career to an end. For this reason it might be wise to insure your hearing.

Your premises will also need insuring. If you own them you will need to cover the building for fire and accident and the contents for damage or theft. If you rent premises, make certain that you would not be left with a liability if a fire in your part damaged other people's property. Seeing clients at home may invalidate your policy unless you first advise your insurance company.

Public liability insurance is sometimes included as part of your premises insurance but you should check this. Cover should protect you if a client or other member of the public has an accident on your premises and claims that you were negligent.

Professional indemnity insurance protects you as a professional person. If a client claims that you have acted unethically, that your methods of work have damaged them in some way, this could lead to lengthy legal proceedings. You may be accused of assault or engaging in unsolicited sexual activity with your client. Even if this is totally without foundation, defending against such an action could be very expensive but this cover will ensure that you do not have to pay.

Finally, remember that driving between your home and your consulting room will constitute driving to and from work so check that your car insurance remains valid.

Chapter summary

- Make a risk assessment of every client you plan to see.
- Obtain as a minimum details of their name, address and telephone number.
- Be wary of general advertising and try to accept referrals only from known sources.
- Have a telephone, mobile phone or attack alarm with you during every session.
- Make sure someone can receive a distress call from you if necessary.
- Select a pre-planned code word you can use in distress.
- Do not see clients in an isolated setting, where no-one can come to your aid.
- Consider tape recording sessions with the client's agreement.
- Do not accept close friends, colleagues etc. as clients, but make sure they know how to refer other people to you.
- If you form a personal relationship with a client, do not try to provide a professional relationship simultaneously.
- It is unethical to have a sexual relationship with a client.
- Keep your premises safe.
- Review your insurance requirements.

7

Promoting Private Practice

What kind of practice?

Getting your personal priorities clear right from the start can save a lot of difficulty later. Is your primary aim to make a great deal of money or to offer counselling as a service to others? Do you accept that some clients will be able to pay the full price while others will never be able to afford to? Is your aim to bring in a little extra income on top of another job, or will your income need to support a family and pay for a pension?

Once you have addressed these questions, you will have a clear idea of the size of practice you aim to develop. This in turn will help to clarify how much effort you will need to put into marketing.

Understanding the market-place

It may seem strange at first to think of a competitive market-place for the provision of therapy, in much the same way as rows of greengrocers' stalls in a market town. This was however brought home to me by my own therapist, who lived a few streets away from me as I was doing my training. One day she pointed out to me that in starting to see clients I was setting up in direct competition to her. Recognising that we are all in competition with one another is an important starting point, sometimes difficult to acknowledge, especially for those who have chosen a caring profession.

Next we need to ask ourselves what is special about our practice. Is it style, theoretical orientation or training? Do you primarily see yourself as a counsellor, a psychotherapist or an analyst? Have a thorough audit of what makes you, and your practice special. When you have done that pause and think. You may know the difference between say a Jungian and a Freudian, but what about your potential clients? Does this trade jargon have the slightest meaning to most of them? I suggest that unless they are seeking a training analysis for themselves as future practitioners, you will need to be ready to explain very clearly what you offer.

What special skills do you bring to your work, what for example is unique about the particular training or specialisms that you have developed? What would mark your practice out as being different from others? Do you for example work in stress management or concentrate on women's issues? Whatever it is you have to offer your clients sets you aside and makes your work special. You should identify this then promote yourself accordingly.

Couple work

Private practice does not only mean seeing people individually. While comments so far have applied primarily to the one-to-one method of working, much has relevance for those practitioners who offer therapy to families, couples or groups. It is of course important to be appropriately trained before branching out into any of these areas, but equally it is important to consider the economic consequences.

Private fees charged for couples work tend to be higher than individual sessions, somewhere between £35 and £70 a session in London, and those sessions are likely to be longer too, perhaps up to an hour-and-a-half. Local branches of Relate often have lengthy waiting lists and may be in a position to make referrals to properly trained couple therapists. However, they may only refer to people who have completed recognised couple training such as their own.

Couples work can be more draining to the therapist because there are three matters to attend to simultaneously, namely the problems of two individual people and their relationship with one another. Therapists who offer psychosexual counselling need specialist training in addition to couples counselling.

Sometimes clients ask whether you will be prepared to see their partner either with them or separately. In such circumstances it is important to clarify three things:

- Are you sufficiently qualified and confident of being able to provide such a service?
- Will you see them individually or as a couple?
- What effect will your current relationship have on the absent partner?

There will inevitably be a sense in which the first client 'owns' you as you are already their therapist and this can set up considerable assumptions and resistance in their partner right from the start. Consider whether the request to see you has actually come from their partner or is it simply a wishful thought on the part of your client? Asking their partner to make contact directly with you will help to clarify this. Alternatively with your client's permission, you could offer to write to them yourself. Sometimes this can be very helpful, demonstrating to the absent partner that you have a professional concern for both of them and for their relationship with one another. On occasions this approach may lead to anger on the part of the absent client. However this can have a positive effect, assisting both to get to the root of their feelings and confirm whether joint counselling or therapy is right for them at this stage.

From a practical point of view you will need premises that are suitable for seeing a couple, perhaps with a sofa and arm chair or at least three chairs. You will have the added complication of getting the three of you together for an appointment rather than just two. A partner who has ambivalent feelings about coming in the first place may cancel appointments or drop out at a later date and there is twice the opportunity for this to happen with a couple. If just one of them turns up for the appointment you will need to think about how to proceed. Should you refuse to see them individually once they have contracted to work as a couple, or will there be occasions when it is right to see one or both of them separately?

In some cases it will be more appropriate to work conjointly with another therapist. One should be allocated to each individual client and the four of you will meet together for sessions as well. Do you have an arrangement with another therapist to provide this? It can take some organising and requires real commitment on everyone's part to make it work. It also requires more complicated room arrangements with the use of two rooms (or at least two different time slots) for the individual work and one room where four people can meet comfortably. If only two rooms are available, then issues of territory and favouritism may arise if you use one of the individual locations for couple work as well.

Groupwork

Self-help groups exist for a variety of purposes. One of the best known examples is Alcoholics Anonymous who base their treatment programme on mutual support through regular attendance at a group. Other types such as psychotherapy groups are facilitated by professional group facilitators. Like couple work this requires specialist training. Groupwork courses are run by organisations such the Institute of Group Analysis and the Westminster Pastoral Foundation where students have the opportunity to learn theory and to experience group dynamics, and the facilitation of groups.

Although groups involve more administration than individual work, they are much more efficient in use of time and consequently more profitable. Take for example a one-and-a-half hour therapy group for eight participants who are charged at £15 per client per session. Allowing for an additional half hour of administration, making two hours in all, such a group would produce an income of £120. It would be necessary to charge the unrealistic fee of £60 an hour to make individual work equally productive.

Networking

To be successful you need a good reputation but arguably you can only have a good reputation if you are successful. Everything you say or do which is picked up by a potential client will add to or subtract from your reputation. This applies to every client session, every article written, even every chance conversation about work at a party. Be certain that everyone you know is aware of the work you do, has respect for your work and is prepared to recommend you to others. Simple in concept but hard to achieve, networking involves using the contacts you already have to develop your business successfully. This will involve building good personal and professional relationships over a long period of time.

Consider what is your current network of contacts; who are the people that you know reasonably well and who might make referrals to you? If you moved into an area ten years ago the chances are by now that you will have had direct and personal contact with hundreds of people, each of whom has their own contacts including family, friends, colleagues and so on. Because all your friends, acquaintances and colleagues will themselves have circles of people whom they relate to, your network can quickly expand to hundreds, possibly thousands of people, each with the potential to be a client or refer one to your practice.

Some examples might be life long contacts such as:

■ relations
■ friends
■ people on your Christmas card list
■ colleagues

Moving into a new area might bring you in contact with:

■ estate agents
■ neighbours
■ shopkeepers
■ hairdressers
■ car mechanics
■ Citizen Advice Bureaux
■ surveyors
■ solicitors
■ neighbours
■ schools
■ churches

Studying for a qualification might bring you into contact with:

■ fellow students
■ lecturers or tutors

An interest in sport or other club activities might bring you into contact with:

■ other team members
■ social club members
■ their families and friends

Health concerns might bring you into contact with:

- dentists
- doctors
- consultants

Unlike someone selling double glazing you will not be able to pick up leads door to door. You will not want to see people who you already know because it is inappropriate to have members of your own family, friends and acquaintances as clients. Every client needs to be at least once removed from your immediate circle of contacts. The majority of counsellors and psychotherapists would probably agree that it is possible to work with someone in a therapeutic relationship only if you have no social contact with them. So while it might just be acceptable to see your partner's hairdresser or golfing tutor, you should avoid seeing someone you know directly from the pub or the baby sitting circle – refer them on to someone else instead. While you will never be offering counselling or psychotherapy directly to anyone that you already know these people should nevertheless be aware of the work that you do.

Protecting the consumer

Some years ago it was rather frowned upon for any professional such as a solicitor or an accountant to advertise. The thinking was that selling yourself rather cheapened the process of providing a service. By advertising you might imply that you were offering something better than, or at least different from that offered by your colleagues in other firms. A brass plate was just about acceptable, but large advertisements in telephone directories and local newspapers were not deemed appropriate by professional bodies.

Over the past twenty years, however, there has been a change in the expectations held towards professionals. Political changes have helped to develop a market economy which places emphasis on choice and value for money (and real choice can only be available where there is a certain amount of advertising permitted). The public have demanded much more information about the services they receive. Solicitors may now advertise their specialities, for example in conveyancing, marital or employment matters. Doctors have been encouraged to explain (for example in leaflets directed at their patients) any specialist services they offer such as ante-natal care and well-woman clinics. The risk in all this however is that professional service providers may be tempted to make exaggerated claims about how their service is better than that provided by others.

A Code of Ethics and Practice is one means of ensuring that subscribing organisations or individuals protect their clients by working to an agreed standard. Like doctors, solicitors and accountants, many counsellors and psychotherapists belong to professional bodies and thereby subscribe to such a Code. This prevents them from making wide reaching claims about the efficacy of their work in their advertising. For example, The British Association for Counselling *Code of Ethics and Practice for Counsellors* states that counsellors 'should limit the information to name, relevant qualifications, address, telephone number, hours available, and a brief listing of the services offered'. The Institute of Psychotherapy and Counselling in its code, states that 'such statements should be descriptive but not evaluative'. This openness can prove helpful to consumers, patients, clients, and so on as it provides choice but should not lead to unjustifiable claims.

So while counselling and psychotherapy are not as yet professions regulated or recognised by government in the same way as the British Medical Association regulates the activities of doctors, it is nevertheless prudent to restrict any advertising to basic details about the service provided rather than claims of any particular efficacy.

Leaflets and business cards

Before spending money on designing and distributing printed material, stop and think carefully about how you will use it. With an ever increasing tide of circulars, letterboxes are regularly stuffed with junk mail. But would you make an appointment to see a therapist who used blanket coverage in this way? These probably are not the best ways of bringing in this type of business. You will need business cards which show your name, qualification, practice address and telephone number. If you have an answering machine for when you are busy, say so on the card. Have them produced not bigger than a credit card so they will fit easily in a wallet or handbag, keeping the design plain and clear.

Next you will need some leaflets, setting out the type of service you offer, What does that leaflet need to include? The name, address and contact telephone number for your business should be there of course. But you will also need to explain the service you provide and print a map of the area where you work. If you copy an existing map you will need to clarify copyright arrangements for this with the publisher. It should show local train and bus routes as well as local landmarks that make it easier to find you.

Next you will need a short explanation of what you see counselling or psychotherapy to be. Include a brief description of the style of counselling or psychotherapy in which you work and the details of any professional body, Code of Ethics or Complaints Procedure to which you are committed. One effective style is to use a series of questions such as 'Who comes to counselling? What is counselling? How much does it cost? and so on. Here is an example of an initial leaflet, you may wish to include some of these suggestions in your literature.

Name, Qualifications
Address
Telephone number

What service is offered?
Psychodynamic Counselling for people with personal and emotional problems.

What is counselling?
Counselling is the provision of a special relationship with a trained person who will help you to explore difficulties and problems in your life. Many people find that talking things through with someone who has been trained to listen and to support them leaves them less confused and better able to make the changes which they need to improve the quality of their lives.

Who comes for counselling?
All of us go though periods when life seems to lose its meaning. Memories of the past, painful events in the present and worries about the future can all make it difficult to cope with everyday life. Sometimes people are lonely, anxious or depressed, worried about their relationships, their marriage or family life or they may be suffering from bereavement, divorce or separation. Some may want to learn to relate more easily to others or may be looking for more meaning in life.

What qualifications do I have?

I am a Member of the Association/Institute of .... I am bound by their Code of Ethics. This means that in the unlikely event of you wishing to make a complaint about me you have the right to have it independently investigated by them. Their address is ....

Where do I work?

I offer consultations in a quiet, soundproofed private office. I have my own entryphone buzzer which is clearly labelled but it is not obvious from the street that you will be visiting a counsellor. There is no receptionist to go through. It is situated in a busy high street and well lit at night. Although it is on the first floor there is a lift and all doorways are wheelchair accessible. Bus numbers 1, 2 and 3 pass the door and Norton Station is three minutes walk away.

What happens if you make an appointment?

Firstly I will see you for an initial interview. This is an opportunity for us to meet and decide whether my services are of help to you and whether you wish to book further appointments. There is no obligation to book further appointments at the time of your first visit. Indeed many people quite rightly take time thinking carefully about their choice of counsellor. You should allow between an hour and an hour-and-a-half for your first appointment.

What does it cost?

My normal fee is £XX per session. Each appointment lasts fifty minutes. This is payable either in cash at the end of each session or by monthly cheque in response to an invoice. I charge the same fee for initial appointments although these may last longer than fifty minutes if necessary. In cases of financial hardship I am able to see up to two half-fee clients in any one week but this facility is very popular and there may be a considerable wait for an appointment. There is a full fee payable for missed appointments without notice and there is a half fee for all other missed times including sickness and planned holidays. I take three weeks holiday in the summer, one week at Christmas and one at Easter. You will not be asked to pay for these weeks.

How do you contact me?

Please telephone or write to me at the above address and there is a map at the end of the leaflet.

(Include a map)

Local newspapers

Cultivate the local press keeping them informed of the opening and the development of your practice. Include details of any specialist services you offer. But remember local free papers may only have a couple of journalists working at their news desk. Both free and paid-for local papers may promote themselves as services to the community but they are primarily commercial operations geared to selling advertising space. Consequently you cannot expect to get regular free advertising. It is the articles which capture public attention and fill the space between advertisements. So any information that you want published needs to be presented in an exciting way, grabbing the attention of journalists and making the basis of a good story for their readers.

If you issued a press release at Christmas stating 'Psychoanalytic Psychotherapist Opens New Depression Clinic' it might well be binned by the editor, whereas one released a couple of weeks before National No Smoking Day and headed 'New Stress Clinic Helps People Give Up Smoking' is far more likely to catch an editor's eye.

But do you really want publicity at any cost, or would you rather pay for a clear advertisement promoting your practice? Remember it is controversy which excites readers, ignites the letters pages and thereby increases circulation. Sadly any story about mental health issues (especially someone seeing clients in a residential area) can quickly and cruelly be misrepresented, whipping up fears in the community about the presence of mentally disturbed people. Writing your own press release will mean that there is a clear record of what you have said and you could take the advice of at least one MP who always tape records any conversation he has with journalists.

Radio

Local radio stations, especially the smaller ones outside the main conurbations, may well be interested if you have a real story to tell. The opening of a new practice may warrant only a brief news story. But you may be able to feature in a magazine programme. Unless it is a specialist feature, be prepared for a very short interview. Spend ten minutes talking to a reporter and the chances are that this will be edited down to just a few seconds.

Try to get invited in to a programme with phone-ins from listeners. Like counselling and psychotherapy, talk programmes including phone-in shows rely on conversation. A marriage counsellor's views on the latest royal divorce might be relevant to discussions on the future of the monarchy, but it is unlikely to provide a forum for promoting your practice. If however you offer a specialisation that no one else offers locally, you will want to get this across.

Try to promote an interest in what you offer. You are not selling actual sessions which would sound rather crass on the air. If you can handle calls on the air so much the better. You might be invited back to present a programme yourself.

Listen in regularly and find out who presents the 'agony aunt or uncle' feature at the moment. When are they on holiday, who does the programme director use in their place? You will be paid little for a regular slot on local radio, but if handled well it will promote you in your area as a caring and concerned professional. You will be giving the listeners a sense of your professional approach and your ability to help people with problems. Not everyone who uses a radio phone-in will want to seek a face to face interview, however the general publicity for you and your practice will stand you in good stead.

Remember radio listenership always peaks around breakfast time and then tails off throughout the day, rises again at 'drive time' (about 5 pm to 6 pm) and declines again as people turn to television in the evening. Counselling programmes are sometimes late at night so ask yourself whether this is an effective use of your time which will assist you in promoting your practice.

Television

Only national or multinational companies can afford the high advertising fees demanded by most commercial television stations. While advertising is therefore outside the scope of individual practitioners you may nevertheless have something interesting to say about your work. TV producers and programme makers are sometimes interested in a good counselling story but be careful not to be set up. Stories of complaints, unethical behaviour and the like are much more likely to appeal to programme makers than the opening of a new practice. Both BBC and ITV companies have regional news services. Some cable TV companies also provide local news programmes and while the viewing audience may not be great as yet, it is an area set to develop. They cover areas which are more local than the ITV companies but may have just a few thousand regular viewers.

Referrals from doctors

Doctors have plenty of people coming to them with emotional and relationship problems. However, a number of counsellors and psychotherapists that I spoke to while writing this book said that they had tried without success to obtain referrals from GPs. Doctors are often the first port of call for anyone in distress who may feel depressed, anxious, or simply 'under the weather'. However, doctors are also very busy people:

> *Richard was starting up in private practice as a counsellor. He phoned the local health authority and obtained a list of all the GPs in his area. He sent out ninety five letters but received no referrals at all. When he followed up the letters with a telephone call he was given a variety of responses such as: 'We counsel our own patients here', 'We refer people to the community mental health team' and even 'I don't believe in counselling'.*

It is perhaps understandable that with just five or ten minutes to spend with each person and a waiting room full of patients, some doctors will opt for a prescription as the fastest solution available to them. However, many GPs now work in fund-holding practices where they are beginning to realise that it can be more cost effective to employ a practice counsellor or make referrals to a psychotherapist than to provide repeat prescriptions over a long period of time.

Jemima, a psychotherapist who had been a GP receptionist in the past, said:

> *You have to persevere. Doctors receive bundles of mail every day and your leaflets will be lost amongst the free gifts and other inducements from the drug companies. Write to the individual GPs unless there is a practice manager who co-ordinates the work of the practice. Your aim should be to arrange a meeting with all the GPs in the practice to explain what you can offer. Do they have a*

weekly business meeting you could attend? Be clear what you want to offer, whether you are simply seeking referrals to your private practice or might be prepared to see clients on surgery premises. Can you offer a bespoke service for this practice? Regular work by the hour paid for from the practice budget will not be as profitable as private client work but it could be more reliable, so negotiate a reduced fee for surgery work in return for private referrals. Build a relationship, keeping the GPs aware of what you offer and how you work, perhaps sending them regular newsletters when you have something to say or producing personalised leaflets for display within their practice.

GPs may be well trained in listening skills and attempt to provide counselling within the context of ordinary appointments. But because these appointments tend to be so short (nothing like the fifty minutes available in private practice) it is almost inevitable that their pressure of work will make it impossible for any significant work to be done.

Another group of doctors recognise that counselling and psychotherapy is a profession, quite distinct from medicine or even psychiatry. These are the GPs who are prepared to make referrals, provided the experience and training of the practitioner is sufficient.

Larry wanted to develop his psychotherapy practice and had a good friend Ahmed who was also a GP. Cynical at first about the effects of psychotherapy, Ahmed nevertheless changed his mind when one of his patients told him that her mother had had a great deal of help from Larry with her depression. Ahmed invited Larry to speak to other GPs in the practice and as a result of this Larry was invited to provide a counselling clinic direct at their practice one day a week.

The attitude of the person making the referral, in this case a GP, is an essential point to consider. Remember doctors receive huge amounts of information daily, especially from drug companies who have realised that the only way they get their names remembered is to inscribe them on free gifts that might sit on the GP's desk.

You could ask your local Family Practitioner Committee to distribute leaflets to all the GPs in your area but this is a poor substitute for knowing a few doctors personally. Besides, a single communication will not build up a reputation. It is far better to spend time cultivating a personal relationship with the people who are likely to make referrals than simply sending literature, unless you are prepared to spend large sums of money producing regular communications such as a newsletter outlining the development of the service you offer over time.

So before you go to the expense of printing literature, be certain how it will be used. Will leaflets actually be made available in doctors' waiting rooms as well as other locations such as dentists, hospital outpatients' waiting rooms, clinics, libraries and other public areas? How many can you realistically distribute, bearing in mind both your budget and the time involved in distribution? Providing fifty for each doctor in your area may be an expensive operation with the risk that they will simply get lost in the back of a cupboard. Sometimes a co-operative approach with another practitioner can be effective:

Gillian, a counsellor with a developing private practice in a South London suburb, approached her own GP who was willing to make referrals to her. Gillian realised that she would not be able to see all the clients referred because some might be her neighbours and other people known to her. So she linked up with Brenda, another counsellor who lived two miles away and who had a similar arrangement with her local GP. In that way they were able to provide a service to both GPs and refer clients to one another when necessary. This common approach eventually led to them forming a partnership and sharing supervision arrangements. Both doctors are now confident about making referrals.

Working with doctors

Of course not all mental health problems can be cured by therapy alone. There are many occasions when a course of drug treatment from the client's GP can provide early relief from symptoms. Antidepressants over a short period of time, for example, may lift a client's mood sufficiently for them to make constructive use of therapy (Daines et al., 1997).

Charles had a new practice as a psychotherapist and his first appointment was to see a new client called Samantha. Both sat in virtual silence for fifty minutes. Keen to be client-centred and understanding this to mean that he should not lead the client in any way, Charles simply waited for the client to speak. Samantha however was deeply depressed following two sudden deaths in her family. Charles never found this out and after a second session Samantha decided not to come again.

Had Charles been able to engage his client more fully, he might have discovered that she had a history of depression which had been successfully treated with medication. If her doctor had prescribed the use of a short-term antidepressant this might have enabled her to make use of the sessions. Perhaps it would also have been helpful to have sought the client's permission to talk to her doctor, so that there could have been co-operation in her treatment.

Experience shows that despite training, GPs do vary considerably in their attitudes to psychological matters. Some will see counselling or psychotherapy as a positive benefit, others consider that these matters are best left to the psychiatric services in the NHS. A few will try to offer some form of counselling or therapy themselves, or they may be able to provide access to a counsellor at their practice. Presenting yourself as offering something in addition to existing services will help to raise your profile among local medical professionals.

You should also make contact with local NHS consultant psychiatrists. There are several reasons for this. As part of their training some practitioners are encouraged to seek a training placement, perhaps as an honorary psychotherapist at a psychiatric hospital. This is a good way to gain experience in a wide range of mental health issues and can help in other ways such as providing access to specialist libraries and professional case discussion groups. Such contacts may assist you in finding a consultant psychiatrist for your own practice and generally broaden opportunities to develop knowledge and skills. Finally, some of their patients may be suitable for private psychotherapy or counselling.

Chapter summary

- What unique skills or experience do you offer to clients?
- Know your market-place and competitors.
- Build a network to develop referrals.
- Publish your contact details and descriptive literature.
- Develop a good relationship with the local media.
- GPs may be an important source of referrals.
- Increasing numbers of GPs have a counsellor attached to their practice.

8

Defining Success in Private Practice

Reviewing plans

Successful businesses don't stand still. You need to review regularly what you do and think ahead about how your work will develop. We have seen the advantage of a business plan when it comes to starting up a business or discussing your aims and objectives with your bank manager. Look back at the plan you wrote and see how relevant it is every six months. It is also worthwhile developing a strategy for the next three years and updating this every year. This will relate back to your original business plan, recognise the achievements you have made and redefine goals as your life, your needs and your business develop.

Time management

While client work throughout the profession seems to run to a regular fifty minute clinical hour, how else could you make your use of time more efficient? For example, how far do you travel for supervision, and how much time does that take up? Is it time to review your supervision contract anyway? Some counsellors change their supervisor every two years or so as a matter of course. Unlike therapy, where we might accuse clients of avoidance if they move from one therapist to another, a change of supervisor now and then offers a fresh angle on our clients and provides the opportunity to switch from a male to a female supervisor or vice versa.

Do you lecture or teach, and if so who pays for your preparation time? Would you be better off seeing more clients and doing less lecturing? You will want to balance the need for income against a healthy variety of work, so this is another aspect which you should occasionally review. Your pattern of work might well include occupations that are not directly related to any kind of therapy. A good balance can sometimes be achieved by taking up a hobby, interest or even part-time work that has a physical rather than emotional or psychological aspect to it.

Is your own personal growth in tune with your practice needs? Some well established practitioners believe that they no longer need supervision or personal therapy. Although the British Association for Counselling *Code of Ethics and Practice for Counsellors* stops short of obligatory and continuous personal therapy, ongoing supervision and continued professional development are regarded as ethical requirements (see Appendix 2). When considering your current need for personal development (which may include therapy, further training or additional supervision) remember it will change over time. Some objectivity is called for, so be prepared to listen to others such as your supervisor, therapist, family and colleagues. If you think your therapist is simply trying to keep you in long-term therapy against your will, then a trusted colleague may be a good person to discuss this matter with rather than simply to end without further reflection.

Keeping clients

Discussing whether your therapist can keep clients against their will brings us to consider whether we can all get ourselves caught in this trap. If we are honest, we all have our favourite clients. We would not be human if we didn't find it preferable to spend fifty minutes with someone who amuses, flatters or entertains us than with someone who is in deep depression, angry or dismissive. Of course our role is not to keep clients as such. Once a client chooses to leave, it would be quite wrong to keep them against their will. There may be times when you will be able to interpret a client's desire to finish and possibly further work will be done as a result. But new practitioners especially often wonder why they find it difficult to keep their clients. Do your clients perhaps come for an initial appointment but then not return? Is something putting them off? Could it be your price or location, your personal style or approach, or even your personality? If clients come just once, what does this say about the quality of your assessments? Discuss these matters in supervision and in your own therapy to see if there is anything you can do to change:

Susan set up a counselling practice at home, receiving plenty of referrals from the GP practice where her friend worked as a secretary. She found that many clients came for one or two sessions, but they didn't return to do any ongoing work. Susan had a very warm and outgoing personality. In discussion with her supervisor however, he suggested that she was so keen to offer a good service in her new career that she was putting people off. He picked up a sense that she was desperate for work rather than just keen to provide a good service and suggested that her clients might be experiencing this as well. Consequently clients were scared away. By taking on consultancy work with a counselling centre, she was no longer entirely dependent on her clients for income and could relate in a less anxious manner so allowing her clients to relax and use the sessions better.

When clients sense that their therapist wants to keep them when they themselves feel they no longer want to be there, they can feel trapped and understandably want to free themselves, whatever their ongoing need for therapy may be.

Personal fulfilment

In my discussions with other counsellors and psychotherapists while writing this book I was heartened by the number of people who said the work was very fulfilling. One said:

At times it can be really exhausting, frustrating or down-right depressing. However, I get enormous satisfaction from seeing a client slowly shift and start to deal with the issues that had caused them pain. To end with a client who has really been through the mill, but come out the other side with a new approach to life and a swing in their step is quite magnificent, and worth all the effort of interpretation, empathy and patience necessary in private practice.

Another spoke of the privilege of seeing another person successfully concluding their time in therapy:

True there will be days when it seems rather depressing and we wonder why on earth we do this work. However, there is a privilege in being allowed inside another person's world to share in an intimate way those moments of rich insight. It can be a really humbling experience and one which keeps many of us at it for year upon year.

Burnout

Anyone who is self-employed has only themselves to set standards of hours worked and value given. With no-one else to measure against, it can be difficult to set realistic targets for achievement. Ministers of religion and members of parliament are in similar positions, where the amount of work they engage in is almost entirely at their own discretion. The danger for any self-employed person is that they become so concerned about keeping their business going that they put financial survival above all other considerations (see Feltham, 1995b).

Eric was in private practice as a marital counsellor but never seemed to find the time to have a holiday. Eight years went by, and his health and own marriage started to suffer. He had convinced himself that he needed to work every day if he was to make a success of his practice, not recognising that he was actually very successful already. A mild heart attack forced him to take stock of what he was doing and a period of personal therapy (which he thought he did not have the time for) helped him to see that he could charge higher fees and reduce his working hours to make life more comfortable.

Starting or joining a practitioners' group

Eric was rather isolated with little contact with other practitioners. Had he been meeting in a peer group of other practitioners he might have found help in addressing these matters earlier on. You might consider contacting others who are in practice locally if there is not already a local group you could join. People will probably have been through different training and come from different theoretical standpoints and at first this may seem strange. Although you may disagree with other people's style of work you may nevertheless learn from one another. Some such groups are strictly for peer group support while others agree to appoint a facilitator. This is not a substitute for supervision but an additional resource which can help everyone in the development of their practice. People who have trained together sometimes maintain their links, meeting purely socially or setting aside time for reflection on their work. Others meet more formally and share professional papers in a discussion group. All these activities can help to break down the potential isolation of work in private practice.

Other uses of supervision

Supervision need not always be used to address issues pertaining to individual clients. It is a legitimate use of supervision from time to time to take an overview of your career or your relationship to your practice. This may help prevent things from going wrong, giving you opportunities to think whether you have enough or too many clients, whether you are getting personal satisfaction from your work or whether you are feeling burnt out by it. Perhaps you could set aside a supervision session once a quarter in order to discuss these matters. Hiding your feelings about your work (rather like being ashamed of failure at school) will not help you, nor in the long run will it help your supervisor to help you either.

When things go wrong

Even with the best supervision and personal planning of your career things can still go wrong, so what should you do if you find that you are not enjoying your work, or it makes you tired or irritable? It can be very distressing for a counsellor or psychotherapist who has built their life and their income around private practice to find they are questioning whether they really want to go on earning their living in this way. For some this may lead to a fresh challenge but more than likely for many others it will arouse fear and anxiety. Many of us come into this kind of work after a period of distress in our own lives, indeed it is often empathy drawn from this that enables us to listen to and understand others.

However, circumstances change for all of us and what was an ideal career ten years ago may no longer provide the satisfaction required now.

If this is your experience, take some time to think about why this is. First stop should be to discuss this with your supervisor, for it is in the interests of both you and your clients to understand why you are feeling this way. It could be that one or more of your clients have dealt with their feelings by projecting them on to you, so maybe you need some help in order to disentangle yourself from this. There may be other stresses going on in your own life such as children leaving (or not leaving!) home, elderly parents who need care, financial worries or relationship problems. It may seem to be stating the obvious but counsellors and psychotherapists are most certainly not immune from ordinary life issues like these.

Your supervisor may advise you to consider having some personal therapy for yourself, or if you are already in therapy to consider these issues there. This should not be considered a criticism, indeed working on a particular issue may be a worthwhile investment for your practice as well as for you as an individual. As a result you may be able to recover and continue. Remember the professional in this kind of work is someone who is always prepared to reflect on their ability to do the work and then act accordingly. It is not a failure to cancel a session when you have a migraine or to suspend your practice while you cope with a close personal bereavement. These are the more honest and ethical responses. But carrying on as if nothing had happened is likely to be damaging both to your clients and to your reputation.

If having talked these things through carefully you recognise that you have really had enough of listening to others for a living you may well need to withdraw from this kind of work, at least for a while. Think carefully about the effect that this will have on your life, your finances and so on and try to approach this in a planned way. You may feel able to reduce your workload rather than stop completely. You may like to view retirement not as a specific date in the future but as a gradual running down of your practice over a period of time. If you decide not to accept referrals remember that it will take several years to get your name out of directories and there will always be old copies around. Think about to whom you would want to refer existing or potential clients.

Publicity

Practitioners fail to obtain or retain clients for several reasons. People may not know about the service because it has not been sufficiently advertised or promoted, the price may be too high, the business may have a poor reputation or there may simply be no demand for the service offered in that location, perhaps because there are other practitioners already successfully operating or because there are other avenues of effective support available to people.

Have your attempts to publicise your service been successful, in other words do people actually know what you have to offer? Some additional research might be called for. This need not be complicated or expensive but you do need to find out whether local people who might be expected to make referrals to you are actually aware of how to put clients in contact with you. Something as simple as a wrong telephone number passed on can make people give up and go elsewhere, so take the opportunity to make sure that your literature is completely up to date.

Remember that word of mouth plays a crucial role in developing a professional reputation. You should take every opportunity to improve your network of contacts by attending professional meetings with colleagues and others who might make referrals to you.

If you provide leaflets in bulk for distribution, for example in waiting rooms, you will need to visit regularly to top them up. It is a good idea to purchase plastic display stands for leaflets bearing your telephone number so that requests for more can be dealt with promptly.

It may be that it is price that is proving an obstacle to potential clients. Look again at what competitors are charging, especially those that are local to you. If you are a psychotherapist you may feel that a psychotherapy training entitles you to charge more than someone who promotes themselves as a counsellor, however if that person is cheaper, more effective at promoting their practice and say, nearer to the local station, they may well be in a better position to charge higher fees. You should in any case regularly review your fees, the way you present your service to potential clients and possibly your location. Consider this from a client's perspective. Is there anything about the location of your practice that makes it less likely that they will come to you? Is it a safe part of town, or easy enough to find if it is out of town? Is it in a well lit area where people would not be afraid to venture out at night (even if you only see clients during the day)? Is it accessible by public transport and easy enough to park? Does it have its own parking or are the local parking facilities secure and safe enough for people travelling alone? Is it obvious from the street name plate or sign that anyone calling is seeking some form of therapy or could they be simply visiting any office?

Competition

Think about the full range of competitors that you are up against, not just local private practitioners. Consider these examples:

- Local GPs may see themselves as providers of brief counselling.
- The local branch of Relate will be seeing individuals as well as couples.
- Counselling centres run by charitable trusts will seek donations from clients, effectively charging less than your private fees.
- There may be other people advertising private practices.
- Local NHS psychiatric services will be free, stretched in their ability to meet demand but providing services to people who are unsuitable for or could not afford private therapy.
- Social services are over stretched, sometimes offering brief counselling but again only for people who cannot afford private services.
- Youth counselling services are sometimes funded by parental donations.
- Local self-help groups may be free or only require a small donation.
- Victim Support schemes are free to victims.

Budget

Look again at your budget. Were your calculations realistic or optimistic? It could be that some of the estimates of what you would earn were over generous, or that your expenses have risen faster than you expected. Keep an eye on the rate of inflation, because this will indicate how much additional profit you will need to develop each year just to maintain the same standard of living.

You should rarely need to increase fees for existing clients. Consider instead simply deciding your fee rate for new clients at the beginning of each year. As clients paying the old rate leave, new ones should take their place, paying at the new rate. It is true that clients who have been with you for several years will be paying slightly less than the current rate but this should be compensated for by the fact that they are a regular and reliable source of income.

Protecting clients if you cannot work

I once had to turn a client away on the door step. I knew she had travelled several miles to see me but I had such a splitting headache at the time that I would have been little or no use to her at all. Sometimes we just have to say 'No', and it is far better to be honest with our clients. I once charged a client only half a fee because I knew I was falling asleep during the session and that on that occasion it was definitely me who needed the sleep; I'm certain it wasn't just an effect of the counter-transference! But what if a practitioner is seriously ill or incapacitated by an accident, or even dies during the course of work with a client? We need to be responsible in our dealings with clients so as to ensure that the minimum amount of distress is caused to them if we are unable to function.

A sealed envelope containing contact details of your clients should be left with another nominated practitioner (some professional bodies insist on this). This needs to be updated regularly and should only be opened in the event of your death, sudden illness or other unusual event which prevented you from contacting your clients and continuing to work with them. There are some clients who will not like the idea of any information, however secure, being made available to a third party. However on balance this is a caring thing to do and would usually be accepted as such. There is no suggestion that your client would automatically continue with the other person, (and this needs to be made clear) but they would simply receive the offer of help in dealing with the situation. This assistance should normally be provided free of charge. It may mean a referral elsewhere or an end to therapy altogether but at least these matters would not need to be faced by your clients in isolation (see Traynor and Clarkson, 1992).

Ending your practice

It is responsible to plan for the ending of your practice because depressing as it may seem, we all retire at some stage and eventually die. Some of us simply need to change jobs or move home from time to time. It is far better if clients can be prepared for this. I have stressed that many business issues around private practice are similar for both counsellors and psychotherapists. However, it would not be good practice to take on a long-term client knowing that you were planning to retire or move away in the near future. Of course people's circumstances change. Marriage, pregnancy, illness, caring responsibilities or bereavement can all affect our practice as well our personal lives. Practitioners will sometimes need to withdraw from this work, either temporarily or permanently, and it is a measure of professional competence rather than failure to recognise when this is necessary. Our clients cannot be totally sheltered from the effect of these things anymore than we can, but some medium and long-term planning will ensure that work with clients is disrupted as little as possible.

Clients who are not ready to end therapy may have to do so when you reach retirement or if you decide to pursue a different career. These situations need to be handled sensitively. If at all possible, you should give adequate notice of your intention to end. This may not be possible if you are ill or otherwise incapacitated, nevertheless you should still try to plan with your clients individually how you will finish. Try to think about this in advance, so that you do not take on any new long-term clients shortly before finishing. Perhaps a month or two's notice is sufficient for clients of less than a year's duration, maybe up to three months for longer term clients, although this will to some extent depend on your relationship with each client.

It is very important that clients understand clearly why you are finishing. Use the time by all means to help your clients work through the inevitable feelings of loss (or maybe relief!). But saying something like 'I am finishing in private practice to retire to the country' or 'I am moving to a new employed post in the North' is far more honest than leaving clients to wrestle with their fantasies. If this is not explained properly, some will imagine that their problems have been too much for you to bear. Others may exhibit many of the features we expect to find in someone who is bereaved, perhaps crying and telling you how much they will miss you, perhaps being angry or ending sooner to avoid the planned ending you have arranged. Be prepared for a difficult time and consider doubling up the amount of personal supervision you have available.

Conclusion

Counselling or psychotherapy in private practice provides reward-ing and stimulating work for many people. It is a career many enjoy. Despite isolated cases of abuse and occasional criticism of the professions in the media, the vast majority of clients gain considerable benefit from talking through their difficulties with a professional who is ready to listen and understand.

In this book I have tried to set out some of the practical matters to consider before embarking on this type of work. It is hard to pick out the most important points to consider when starting out in private practice as a counsellor or psychotherapist, but in taking an overview at the end it occurs to me everyone should start with a good professional training and supervised experience of casework. To succeed you will need to feel comfortable work-ing in relative isolation and marketing yourself. Subscribing to a recognised code of ethics and an independent complaints pro-cedure will help give your clients confidence in you and the service you offer.

Consider your finances carefully before embarking on private practice, remembering that many small businesses fail in their first year. Consult experts and seek advice from others. Without a steady and growing source of clients you will have no income, so plan carefully how you will obtain those all important referrals. Keep your accounts in good order and set aside your income tax as you earn. Deal fairly with your clients and build a good relationship with colleagues and other professionals who may make referrals to you. Knowing your limitations and being pre-pared to make referrals to other specialists will help to build these relationships further.

Ensure that you have a comfortable pleasant environment in which to see your clients. If you use a room at home then consider the effect upon your family. Make sure it is sound-proofed. Promote your business well, keeping your literature up to date and well distributed but using personal contact to develop referral networks wherever possible. Write clear notes and keep them in a secure place. Make good use of supervision and psychiatric consultation on a regular basis. Finally, take time out regularly to reflect on your business plans.

I cannot pretend to have successfully completed all the tasks in this book myself, because improving and developing a practice is a never-ending process. I hope however that I have provided information and ideas which will prove useful as you develop your practice in the months and years ahead. Enjoy the work!

Appendix 1:

Personal Financial Plan

1. Your home:

Mortgage or rent ....

Life assurance ....

Mortgage protection insurance ....

Home maintenance ....

Council tax ....

Gas ....

Electricity ....

Water and sewerage ....

Home telephone ....

TV licence/cable/satellite TV ....

Sub-total 1. ....

2. Yourself and your family:

Food shopping ....

Take aways ....

Meals out ....

Newspapers/magazines ....

Laundry/dry cleaning ....

School dinners ....

School trips ....

Clothes adults ....

Clothes children ....

Personal requisites ....

Holidays away ....

Birthdays/festivals ....

Confectionery ....

Alcohol ....

Clubs/subscriptions ....

Charity donations ....

Adult personal spending allowance ....

Children's pocket money ....

Savings account ....

Loan, catalogue and credit cards ....

Sub-total 2. ....

3. Travelling:

Train, bus and taxi fares ....

Season ticket or loan ....

Car/motorcycle tax ....

Car/motorcycle insurance ....

MOT ....

Servicing ....

Petrol/oil/parking ....

Breakdown membership ....

Allowance for vehicle depreciation ....

Sub-total 3. ....

Total (1. + 2. + 3.) ....

Appendix 2:

British Association for Counselling Code of Ethics and Practice for Counsellors

1.   Status of this code
1.1   In response to the experience of members of the British Associ-
      ation for Counselling, this code is a revision of the 1993 code.

2.   Introduction
2.1   The purpose of this code is to establish and maintain standards
      for counsellors who are members of the British Association for
      Counselling and to inform and protect members of the public
      seeking and using their services.

2.2   All members of this Association are required to abide by the
      existing codes appropriate to them. They thereby adopt a com-
      mon frame of reference within which to manage their respons-
      ibilities to clients, colleagues, members of this Association and
      the wider community. While this code cannot resolve all ethical
      and practice related issues, it aims to provide a framework for
      addressing ethical issues and to encourage optimum levels of
      practice. Counsellors will need to judge which parts of this code
      apply to particular situations. They may have to decide between
      conflicting responsibilities.

2.3   The Association has a Complaints Procedure which can lead to the expulsion of members for breaches of its Codes of Ethics and Practice.

3.   The Nature of Counselling

3.1   The overall aim of counselling is to provide the opportunity for the client to work towards living in a more satisfying and resourceful way. The term 'counselling' includes work with individuals, pairs or groups of people often, but not always, referred to as clients. The objectives of particular counselling relationships will vary according to the client's needs. Counselling may be concerned with developmental issues addressing and resolving specific problems, making decisions, coping with crisis, developing personal insight and knowledge, working through feelings of inner conflict, or improving relationships with others. The counsellor's role is to facilitate the client's work in ways which respect the client's values, personal resources and capacity for self-determination.

3.2   Only when both the user and the recipient explicitly agree to enter into a counselling relationship does it become counselling rather than the use of counselling skills.

3.3   It is not possible to make a generally accepted distinction between counselling and psychotherapy. There are well founded traditions which use the terms interchangeably and others which distinguish them. Regardless of the theoretical approaches preferred by individual counsellors, there are ethical issues which are common to all counselling situations.

4.   The Structure of this Code
          This code has been divided into two parts. The Code of Ethics outlines the fundamental values of counselling and a number of general principles arising from these. The Code of Practice applies these principles to the counselling situation.

A.   CODE OF ETHICS

A.1   Counselling is a non-exploitative activity. Its basic values are integrity, impartiality and respect. Counsellors should take the same degree of care to work ethically whether the counselling is paid or voluntary.

A.2   Client Safety
          All reasonable steps should be taken to ensure the client's safety during counselling.

A.3   Clear Contracts
          The terms in which counselling is being offered should be made clear to clients before counselling commences. Subsequent revision of these terms should be agreed in advance of any change.

A.4 Competence
Counsellors should take all reasonable steps to monitor and develop their own competence and to work within the limits of that competence. This includes having appropriate and ongoing counselling supervision/consultative support.

B. CODE OF PRACTICE

B.1 Introduction
This code applies these values and ethical principles to more specific situations which may arise in the practice of counselling.

B.2 Issues of Responsibility:
B.2.1 The counsellor–client relationship is the foremost ethical concern, but it does not exist in social isolation. For this reason the counsellor's responsibilities to the client, to themselves, colleagues, other members of the Association and members of the wider community are listed under separate headings.

B.2.2 To the Client:

Client Safety
2.2.1 Counsellors should take all reasonable steps to ensure that the client suffers neither physical nor psychological harm during the counselling.

2.2.2 Counsellors do not normally give advice.

Client Autonomy
2.2.3 Counsellors are responsible for working in ways which promote the client's control over his/her own life and respect the client's ability to make decisions and change in the light of his/her own beliefs and values.

2.2.4 Counsellors do not normally act on behalf of their clients. If they do, it will be only at the express request of the client, or else in the exceptional circumstances detailed in B.4.

2.2.5 Counsellors are responsible for setting and monitoring boundaries between the counselling relationship and any other kind of relationship and making this explicit to the client.

2.2.6 Counsellors must not exploit their clients financially, sexually, emotionally, or in any other way. Engaging in sexual activity with the client is unethical.

2.2.7 Clients should be offered privacy for counselling sessions. The client should not be observed by anyone other than their counsellor(s) without having given his/her informed consent. This also applies to audio/video taping of counselling sessions.

Pre-Counselling Information

2.2.8　Any publicity material and written and oral information should reflect accurately the nature of the service on offer and the training, qualifications, and relevant experience of the counsellor (see also B.6).

2.2.9　Counsellors should take all reasonable steps to honour undertakings offered in their pre-counselling information.

Contracting

2.2.10　Clear contracting enhances and shows respect for the client's autonomy.

2.2.11　Counsellors are responsible for communicating the terms on which counselling is being offered, including availability, the degree of confidentiality offered and their expectation of clients regarding fees, cancelled appointments and any other significant matters. The communication of terms and any negotiation over these should be concluded before the client incurs any financial liability.

2.2.12　It is the client's choice whether or not to participate in counselling. Reasonable steps should be taken in the course of the counselling relationship to ensure that the client is given an opportunity to review the terms on which counselling is being offered and the methods of counselling being used.

2.2.13　Counsellors should avoid unnecessary conflicts of interest and are expected to make explicit to the client any relevant conflicts of interest.

2.2.14　If records of counselling sessions are kept, clients should be made aware of this. At the client's request information should be given about access to these records, their availability to other people and the degree of security with which they are kept (see B.4).

2.2.15　Counsellors have a responsibility to establish with clients what other therapeutic or helping relationships are current. Counsellors should gain the client's permission before conferring with other professional workers.

2.2.16　Counsellors should be aware that computer based records are subject to statutory regulations under the Data Protection Act 1984. From time to time the government introduces changes in the regulations concerning the client's right of access to his/her own records. Current regulations have implications for counsellors working in social service and health care settings.

Counsellor Competence

2.2.17 Counsellors should monitor actively the limitations of their own competence through counselling supervision/consultative support and by seeking the views of their clients and other counsellors. Counsellors should work within their own known limits.

2.2.18 Counsellors should not counsel when their functioning is impaired due to emotional difficulties, illness, disability, alcohol, drugs or for any other reason.

2.2.19 It is an indication of the competence of counsellors when they recognise their inability to counsel a client or clients and make appropriate referrals.

B.2.3 To Former Clients:

2.3.1 Counsellors remain accountable for relationships with former clients and must exercise caution over entering into friendships, business relationships, sexual relationships, training and other relationships. Any changes in relationships must be discussed in counselling supervision. The decision about any change(s) in relationship with former clients should take into account whether the issues and power dynamics present during the counselling relationship have been resolved and properly ended.

2.3.2 Counsellors who belong to organisations which prohibit sex with all former clients are bound by that commitment.

B.2.4 To Self as Counsellor:

2.4.1 Counsellors have a responsibility to themselves and their clients to maintain their own effectiveness, resilience and ability to help clients. They are expected to monitor their own personal functioning and to seek help and/or withdraw from counselling, whether temporarily or permanently, when their personal resources are sufficiently depleted to require this (see also B.3).

2.4.2 Counsellors should have received adequate basic training before commencing counselling and should maintain ongoing professional development.

2.4.3 Counsellors are encouraged to review periodically their need for professional indemnity insurance and to take out such a policy when appropriate.

2.4.4 Counsellors should take all reasonable steps to ensure their own physical safety.

B.2.5 To other Counsellors:

2.5.1 Counsellors should not conduct themselves in their counselling-related activities in ways which undermine public confidence in either their role as a counsellor or in the work of other counsellors.

2.5.2   If a counsellor suspects misconduct by another counsellor which cannot be resolved or remedied after discussion with the counsellor concerned, they should implement the Complaints Procedure, doing so without breaches of confidentiality other than those necessary for investigating the complaint (see B.9).

B.2.6   To Colleagues and Members of the Caring Professions:

2.6.1   Counsellors should be accountable for their services to colleagues, employers and funding bodies as appropriate. The means of achieving this should be consistent with respecting the needs of the client outlined in B.2.2.7, B.2.2.13 and B.4.

2.6.2   Counsellors are encouraged to increase their colleagues' understanding of the counselling role. No colleague or significant member of the caring professions should be led to believe that a service is being offered by the counsellor which is not, as this may deprive the client of the offer of such a service from elsewhere.

2.6.3   Counsellors should accept their part in exploring and resolving conflicts of interest between themselves and the agencies, especially where this has implications for the client (see also B.2.2.13).

B.2.7   To the Wider Community:

Law

2.7.1   Counsellors should work within the law.

2.7.2   Counsellors should take all reasonable steps to be aware of current law affecting the work of the counsellor. A counsellor's ignorance of the law is no defence against legal liability or penalty including inciting or 'counselling', which has a specific legal sense, the commission of offences by clients.

Social Context

2.7.3   Counsellors will take all reasonable steps to take account of the client's social context.

B.3   Counselling Supervision/Consultative Support:

B.3.1   It is a breach of the ethical requirement for counsellors to practise without regular counselling supervision/consultative support.

B.3.2   Counselling supervision/consultative support refers to a formal arrangement which enables counsellors to discuss their counselling regularly with one or more people who have an understanding of counselling and counselling supervision/consultative support. Its purpose is to ensure the efficacy of the counsellor-client relationship. It is a confidential relationship (see also B.4).

B.3.3   Counsellors who have line managers owe them appropriate managerial accountability for their work. The counselling supervisor role should be independent of the line manager role. However where the counselling supervisor is also the line manager, the counsellor should also have access to independent consultative support.

B.3.4   The volume of supervision should be in proportion to the volume of counselling work undertaken and the experience of the counsellor.

B.3.5   Wherever possible, the discussion of cases within supervision/consultative support should take place without revealing the personal identity of the client.

B.3.6   The ethics and practice of counselling supervision/consultative support are outlined further in their own specific code: the Code of Ethics & Practice for the Supervision of Counsellors (see also B.9).

B.4   Confidentiality: Clients, Colleagues and Others:

B.4.1   Confidentiality is a means of providing the client with safety and privacy. For this reason any limitation on the degree of confidentiality offered is likely to diminish the usefulness of the counselling.

B.4.2   Counsellors treat with confidence personal information about clients, whether obtained directly or indirectly or by inference. Such information includes name, address, biographical details and other descriptions of the client's life and circumstances which might result in identification of the client.

B.4.3   Counsellors should work within the current agreement with their client about confidentiality.

B.4.4   Exceptional circumstances may arise which give the counsellor good grounds for believing that the client will cause serious physical harm to others or themselves, or have harm caused to him/her. In such circumstances the client's consent to a change in the agreement about confidentiality should be sought whenever possible unless there are also good grounds for believing the client is no longer able to take responsibility for his/her own actions. Whenever possible, the decision to break confidentiality agreed between a counsellor and client should be made only after consultation with a counselling supervisor or an experienced counsellor.

B.4.5   Any breaking of confidentiality should be minimised both by restricting the information conveyed to that which is pertinent to the immediate situation and to those persons who can provide the help required by the client. The ethical considerations involve balancing between acting in the best interests of the client and in ways which enable clients to resume taking responsibility for their actions, a very high priority for counsellors, and the counsellor's responsibilities to the wider community (see B.2.7 and B.4.4).

B.4.6   Counsellors should take all reasonable steps to communicate clearly the extent of the confidentiality they are offering to clients. This should normally be made clear in the pre-counselling information or initial contracting.

B.4.7   If counsellors include consultations with colleagues and others within the confidential relationship, this should be stated to the client at the beginning of counselling.

B.4.8   Care must be taken to ensure that personally identifiable information is not transmitted through overlapping networks of confidential relationships. For this reason, it is good practice to avoid identifying specific clients during counselling supervision/consultative support and other consultations, unless there are sound reasons for doing so (see B.2.2.14 and B.4.2).

B.4.9   Any agreement between the counsellor and client about confidentiality may be reviewed and changed by joint negotiations.

B.4.10   Agreements about confidentiality continue after the client's death unless there are overriding legal or ethical considerations.

B.4.11   Counsellors hold different views about whether or not a client expressing serious suicidal intentions forms sufficient grounds for breaking confidentiality. Counsellors should consider their own views and practice and communicate them to clients and any significant others where appropriate (see also B.2.6.2).

B.4.12   Special care is required when writing about specific counselling situations for case studies, reports or publication. It is important that the author either has the client's informed consent, or effectively disguises the client's identity.

B.4.13   Any discussion between the counsellor and others should be purposeful and not trivialising.

B.5   Confidentiality in the Legal Process:

B.5.1   Generally speaking there is no legal duty to give information spontaneously or on request until instructed to do so by a court. Refusal to answer police questions is not an offence, although lying could be. In general terms, the only circumstances in which the police can require an answer about a client and when refusal to answer would be an offence, relate to the prevention of terrorism. It is good practice to ask police personnel to clarify their legal right to an answer before refusing to give one.

B.5.2   Withholding information about a crime that one knows has been committed or is about to be committed is not an offence, save exceptionally. Anyone hearing of terrorist activities should immediately take legal advice.

B.5.3 There is no legal obligation to answer a solicitor's enquiry or to make a statement for the purpose of legal proceedings, unless ordered to do so by a court.

B.5.4 There is no legal obligation to attend court at the request of parties involved in a case, or at the request of their lawyers, until a witness summons or subpoena is issued to require attendance to answer questions or produce documents.

B.5.5 Once in the witness box, there is a duty to answer questions when instructed to do so by the court. Refusal to answer could be punished as contempt of court unless there are legal grounds for not doing so. (It has been held that communications between the counsellor and client during an attempt at 'reconciliation' in matrimonial cases are privileged and thus do not require disclosure unless the client waives this privilege. This does not seem to apply to other kinds of cases.)

B.5.6 The police have powers to seize confidential files if they have obtained a warrant from a circuit judge. Obstructing the police from taking them in these circumstances may be an offence.

B.5.7 Counsellors should seek legal advice and/or contact this Association if they are in any doubt about their legal rights and obligations before acting in ways which conflict with their agreement with clients who are directly affected (see also B.2.7.1).

B.6 Advertising/Public Statements:

B.6.1 When announcing counselling services, counsellors should limit the information to name, relevant qualifications, address, telephone number, hours available and a brief listing of the service offered.

B.6.2 All such announcements should be accurate in every particular.

B.6.3 Counsellors should distinguish between membership of this Association and accredited practitioner status in their public statements. In particular, the former should not be used to imply the latter.

B.6.4 Counsellors should not display an affiliation with an organisation in a manner which falsely implies the sponsorship or verification of that organisation.

Directive made by the Management Committee 23 March 1996. Membership of BAC is not allowed to be mentioned by any person or organisation in press advertisements, in telephone directories, on business cards, on letterheads, on brass plates, on plaques etc. BAC members are encouraged to make oral and written statements to the public and potential clients in letters and pre-counselling leaflets. These statements must include the fact that membership of BAC is not a qualification in counselling but means that the individual and where appropriate the organisation, abides by the Codes of Ethics and Practice and is subject to the Complaints Procedure of the British Association for Counselling. Copies of these Codes and the Complaints Procedure are available from BAC.

This directive does not apply to BAC Recognised Courses, BAC Accredited Counsellors, Supervisors, Trainers, and Fellows who receive separate instruction.

B.7   Research:
B.7.1   The use of personally identifiable material gained from clients or by the observation of counselling should be used only after the client has given consent, usually in writing and care has been taken to ensure that consent was given freely.

B.7.2   Counsellors conducting research should use their data accurately and restrict their conclusions to those compatible with their methodology.

B.8   Resolving Conflicts between Ethical Priorities:
B.8.1   Counsellors will, from time to time, find themselves caught between conflicting ethical principles. In these circumstances, they are urged to consider the particular situation in which they find themselves and to discuss the situation with their counselling supervisor and/or other experienced counsellors. Even after conscientious consideration of salient issues, some ethical dilemmas cannot be resolved easily or wholly satisfactorily.

B.8.2   Ethical issues may arise which have not yet been given full consideration. The Standards and Ethics Sub-Committee of this Association is interested in hearing of the ethical difficulties of counsellors, as this helps to inform the discussion regarding good practice.

B.9   The Availability of other Codes and Guidelines Relating to Counselling:
B.9.1   The following codes and procedures have been passed by the Annual General Meetings of the British Association for Counselling:

Code of Ethics & Practice for Counselling Skills applies to members who would not regard themselves as counsellors, but who use counselling skills to support other roles.

Code of Ethics & Practice for the Supervision of Counsellors exists to guide members offering supervision to counsellors and to help counsellors seeking supervision.

Code of Ethics & Practice for Trainers in Counselling & Trainers in Counselling Skills exists to guide members offering training and to help members of the public seeking counselling training.

Complaints Procedure exists to guide members of BAC and their clients resolving complaints about breaches of the Codes of Ethics and Practice.

Copies and other guidelines and information sheets relevant to maintaining ethical standards of practice can be obtained from the British Association for Counselling Office, 1 Regent Place, Rugby CV21 2PJ.

Guidelines also available:

Telephone Helplines: Guidelines for Good Practice is intended to establish standards for people working on telephone helplines (sponsored by British Telecom). Single copies are available from Telephone Helplines Association, 61 Gray's Inn Road, London WC1X 8LT.

© BAC, 1992   Amended AGM September 1993
           (Management Committee addition 1 May 1996).

References

Blower, V. and Rink, V. (1987) 'Counselling in a private practice', *Counselling*, 60: 10–13.

Bond, T. (1993) *Standards and Ethics for Counselling in Action*. London: Sage.

British Association for Counselling (1992) *Code of Ethics and Practice for Counsellors*. Rugby: BAC.

Carroll, M. (1996) *Counselling Supervision: Theory, Skills and Practice*. London: Cassell.

Casement, P. (1985) *On Learning from the Patient*. London: Routledge.

Coltart, N. (1993) *How to Survive as a Psychotherapist*. London: Sheldon Press.

Daines, B., Gask, L. and Usherwood, T. (1997) *Medical and Psychiatric Issues for Counsellors*. London: Sage.

Dryden, W. and Feltham, C. (1995) *Counselling and Psychotherapy: A Consumer's Guide*. London: Sheldon.

Eysenck, H.J. (1992) 'The outcome problem', in W. Dryden and C. Feltham (eds) *Psychotherapy and its Discontents*. Buckingham: Open University Press.

Feltham, C. (1993) 'What are the difficulties in making a living as a counsellor?', in W. Dryden (ed.) *Questions and Answers on Counselling in Action*. London: Sage.

Feltham, C. (1995a) *What is Counselling?* London: Sage.

Feltham, C. (1995b) 'The stresses of counselling in private practice', in W. Dryden (ed.) *The Stresses of Counselling in Action*. London: Sage.

Gray, A. (1984) *An Introduction to the Therapeutic Frame*. London: Routledge.

Guy, J.D. (1987) *The Personal Life of the Psychotherapist*. New York: Wiley.

James, I. and Palmer, S. (eds) (1996) *Professional Therapeutic Titles: Myths and Realities*. Leicester: British Psychological Society.

Jenkins, P. (1997) *Counselling, Psychotherapy and the Law*. London: Sage.

McMahon, G. (1994) *Starting Your Own Private Practice*. Cambridge: National Extension College.

Mace, C. (ed.) (1995) *The Art and Science of Assessment in Psychotherapy*. London: Routledge.

Maeder, T.C. (1990) *Children of Psychiatrists and Other Psychotherapists*. New York: Harper and Row.

Mowbray, R. (1995) *The Case Against Psychotherapy Registration*. London: Transmarginal Press.

Norton, K. and McGauley, G. (1997) *Counselling Difficult Clients*. London: Sage.

Palmer, S. and McMahon, G. (eds) (1997) *Client Assessment*. London: Sage.

Pilgrim, D. (1993) 'Objections to Private Practice', in W. Dryden (ed.) *Questions and Answers on Counselling in Action*. London: Sage.

Pilgrim, D. (1997) *Psychotherapy and Society*. London: Sage.

Rowan, J. (1988) 'The psychology of furniture', *Counselling*, 64: 21-4.

Shipton, G. (ed.) (1997) *Supervision of Psychotherapy and Counselling: Making a Place to Think*. Buckingham: Open University Press.

Sills, C. (ed.) (1997) *Contracts in Counselling*. London: Sage.

Smith, M.L., Glass, G.V. and Miller, T.I. (1980) *The Benefits of Psychotherapy*. Baltimore, MD: Johns Hopkins University Press.

Syme, G. (1994) *Counselling in Independent Practice*. Buckingham: Open University Press.

Traynor, B. and Clarkson, P. (1992) 'What happens if a psychotherapist dies?', *Counselling* 3 (1): 23-4.

Wilkins, P. (1997) *Personal and Professional Development for Counsellors*. London: Sage.

Useful Addresses

Registration and professional matters

British Association for Counselling
and
United Kingdom Register of Counsellors
1 Regent Place
Rugby, Warwickshire CV21 2PJ
Tel.: 01788 550899

United Kingdom Council for Psychotherapy
167/9 Great Portland Street
London W1N 5FB
Tel.: 0171-436 3002

British Confederation of Psychotherapists
37a Maplesbury Road
London NW2 4HJ
Tel.: 0181-830 5173

British Psychological Society
St. Andrews House
48 Princes Road East
Leicester LE1 7DR
Tel.: 0116-254 9568

Professional indemnity insurance

Smithson Mason Ltd
SMG House
31 Clarendon Road
Leeds LS2 9PA
Tel.: 0113-294 4000

Psychologists' Protection Society
Standalane House
Kincardine
Alloa FK10 4NX
Tel.: 01259 730785

Accountants

Institute of Chartered Accountants in England and Wales
Chartered Accountants' Hall
Moorgate Place
Moorgate
London EC2P 2BJ
Tel.: 0171-920 8682
website: www.icaew.co.uk

Institute of Chartered Accountants in Scotland
27 Queen Street
Edinburgh EH2 1LA
Tel.: 0131-225 5673

Solicitors

The Law Society
113 Chancery Lane
London WC2A 1PL
Tel.: 0171-242 1222

The Law Society of Scotland
26 Drumsheugh Gardens
Edinburgh EH3 7YR
Tel.: 0131-226 7411

Company and computer data registration

Companies House
Crown Way
Cardiff CF4 3UZ
Tel.: 01222 388588

The Office of the Data Protection Registrar
Wycliffe House
Water Lane
Wilmslow
Cheshire SK9 5AF
Tel.: 01625 545740

Learning disabilities

Mencap National Centre
123 Golden Lane
London EC1Y 0RT
Tel.: 0171-454 0454

First aid training

British Red Cross Commercial Training Centre
163 Eversholt Street
London NW1 1DU
Tel.: 0171-388 8777

St John's Ambulance Headquarters
1 Grosvenor Crescent
London SW1X 7EF
Tel.: 0171-235 5231

Personal safety advice

Suzy Lamplugh Trust
14 East Sheen Avenue
London SW14 8AS
Tel.: 0181-392 1839

Index